In Tune with Torah

Meditations for Harmonizing our Lives With God's Torah

———————

Sophia Bar-Lev

In Tune with Torah

ISBN: 978-0-9833994-1-4

Printed in USA by CreateSpace

Dedication

To my beloved children and grandchildren,
May the words of Torah guide you
every day of your lives and
may you always abide
under the shadow of the Almighty.

Table of Contents

Acknowledgements

It is with profound gratitude and respect that I wish to thank and give honor to all who have contributed to the publication of this book.

To my wonderful family for their incomparable love and support for my writing and teaching; to my dear friends who encourage me to keep on keeping on; and to my dear students who give as much or more to me than I have ever given to them.

And most of all, to the Almighty King of the Universe, the Mighty One of Israel whose unconditional love and merciful compassion has graced my life beyond anything I could have imagined. Eternity will not be long enough to give Him sufficient thanks.

May each week's meditation uplift, instruct and encourage every reader and together may our lives create a symphony of praise to the Holy One of Israel as we seek to live each day *In Tune with Torah.*

Sophia Bar-Lev
Tiberias, Israel
Nissan 5772
April 2012

5

Foreword

These are holy words. Perhaps that statement is self-evident; perhaps, in fact, all words are holy. A contemporary poet correctly affirmed "there's a blaze of light in every word," but blessed is the student whose teacher knows how to unlock the sacred illumination contained within.

In the *midrash* collection *Sifrei D'varim* is the extraordinary observation that had Abraham not come into the world it would have been as if – were such a thing possible – God had never existed. When the light is hidden, the darkness is as profound as if it were not there at all.

But when someone can penetrate to the inside and release the illumination within, then even that which is holy already, like the words of Torah, becomes holier still.

My friend and teacher, Sophia Bar-Lev, is someone familiar with the light hidden within. Through her extraordinary years of teaching God's word to willing students of every imaginable perspective, she has gained a deserved reputation as a master of the text. What lifts her above many such teachers is her own willingness to be surprised and transformed by what she herself learns. What endears her to others in the process (and maybe troubles a few!) is her invitation to come along with her on the journey to understanding, wherever it may lead.

If the lessons of Torah were self-evident, there would be no need for Torah. And if the lessons of Torah were unchanging, there would be no need for teachers. *Pirkei Avot* reports Ben Bag-Bag as saying, "Turn it over and over, for everything is in it." And it reports this teaching from Rabbi Joshua ben Perachya: "Find yourself a teacher and make for yourself a companion." This collection of Sophia's teachings will help you tumble the words of Torah and release their light. In making her your teacher, you will find yourself a worthwhile companion.

Enjoy the light.

Rabbi Jack Moline
Agudas Achim Congregation
Alexandria, VA

Beresheit/Genesis

The first book of the Torah

Bersheit

Beresheit/Genesis 1:1 – 6:8

"In the beginning..." The annual Torah reading cycle commences each year immediately after the great festival of Simchat Torah (Rejoicing Over the Torah). In the joyous synagogue service of that special day, the last few verses of Devarim/Deuteronomy are read and followed at once by the first few verses of Beresheit/Genesis to demonstrate the unending cycle of Torah study which has been our privilege for thousands of years.

Included in this parsha is the account of Cain and Abel, the sons of Adam and Eve.

The Rabbis have taught us that three emotions - jealousy, anger and sadness - prevent us from embracing the Divine flow of new life and renewal which Hashem dispenses to His people at the beginning of each new year as a result of our repentance and cleansing on Yom Kippur. Each of these three emotions has the effect of blocking our progress forward in the new year.

Significantly, these three emotions are clearly seen in Cain's relationship with Abel. Although Cain first proposed the idea of bringing an offering to Hashem, when the brothers actually did so, Cain brought an inferior offering while Abel gave his best. When Hashem accepted Abel's offering, the Torah relates that Cain became angry and depressed (sad), which naturally led to jealousy towards his brother.

Hashem reached out to Cain to teach him that all is not lost: *"Surely if you improve, you will be uplifted but if you do not improve, sin crouches at the door; and to you is its desire, yet you can rule over it."* 4:7

In this verse we have encapsulated one of the prevalent teachings of Judaism: 'tikkun olam' - repair of the world, beginning with ourselves.   "If you improve..." Hashem said to Cain, making him to know that failures are never permanent IF we choose to learn from them and improve our inner self.   It was not Cain's inferior offering that was the problem, but the inner attitude that caused him to bring an inferior offering.   This, says Hashem, can be improved, can be overruled.

Our G-d given ability to choose is at the very essence of our being created in the image of Hashem.   The day by day choices we make about what we do or don't do, what we say and don't say, and WHY, are the decisions that weave a pattern of godliness or ungodliness.   A life of spiritual greatness is the sum total of thousands of daily choices motivated by an overruling desire to fulfill the purpose for which we were created: to 'be holy as I am holy' which is Israel's calling and purpose, individually and corporately.

Rashi comments that the phrase "sin crouching at the door" refers to the evil inclination that is always looking to entrap us and other commentators have added that the evil inclination is more interested in the depression that follows sinning than the act itself, for nothing is as spiritually, and even physically, debilitating as depression and sadness.

Jealousy, anger and depression are emotions that affect all of us at one time or another. The question is whether we learn from what Hashem said to Cain, 'you can rule over it' or whether we allow 'it' to rule over us. The choice is ours and we CAN make the right choice, IF we will.

In Tune with Torah: It behooves us early in the new Hebrew year to consider if any unconstructive attitudes or feelings still linger in our minds and emotions, even after Yom Kippur, and if so, recognize that it is never too late to repent and open ourselves to the flow of Divine life and renewal.

Personal Thoughts

Noah

Beresheit/Genesis 6:9 – 11:32

This parsha relates the events surrounding the life of Noah, builder of the ark at Hashem's command. There are some interesting links between Noah and Shabbat.

When Noah was born, his father, Lamech, prophetically exclaimed: *"This one will bring us rest from our work and from the toil of our hands, from the ground which Hashem had cursed."* (Gen. 5:29) The word "Noah" is related to "rest".

Rashi, the eminent Torah commentator, writes that with the advent of Noah on this earth, it became easier to work the earth which had been cursed since Adam ate from the Tree of the knowledge of good and evil in the Garden of Eden. With Noah's birth, concurring closely with Adam's death, the curse was diminished. The invention of the plow is historically attributed to Noah, making agriculture easier. As a result, for the people of that time, the backbreaking and still unproductive labor was eased.

Given the meaning of his name and the measure of 'rest' he brought to mankind, it comes as no surprise that the Zohar links Noah to Shabbat, our day of rest.

Noah happens to be the first person in the Torah who is described as a "tzaddik", a righteous person. In Chassidic writings, a 'tzaddik' is often called 'Shabbat' to express that the state of consciousness of an exceptionally righteous person through the entire week continually draws from and reflects the peace of Shabbat.

This type of person has a deep sense of trust and confidence in Hashem that -- in our everyday language -- keeps him peaceful and calm even in trying and difficult circumstances for his trust in Hashem overrides every earthly care or trial.

Various commentaries allude to the fact that the time Noah and his family spent in the Ark, being carried, as it were, above the turbulent waters of the Flood, is a visual picture of what Shabbat is all about. At the end of each week when we have navigated the unpredictable and often chaotic issues of everyday life, Shabbat grants us rest.

As we all know by experience, there is 'rest' and there is 'rest'. Have not each of us experienced going to bed, for example, and though our body is 'at rest', our mind refuses to shut down and we lay there awake and unable to sleep?

So too with Shabbat. There are two levels of 'rest'.

One of our Sages has commented that it is possible to observe all the instructions regarding Shabbat and still not truly experience Shabbat for an observance based primarily on external do's and don'ts can easily become joyless ritual. True, abiding by the restrictions of Shabbat gives a measure of 'rest', but only by connecting to the spirit of Shabbat in the deepest way do we truly have 'rest'. Restrictions do not make Shabbat - relationship with Hashem makes Shabbat real, alive and full of joy.

Another of the Sages, the Slonimer Rebbe, discusses the symbolism of three levels of the Ark to true observance of Shabbat. He says that the upper floor of the Ark represents our thoughts, the middle floor our speech and the lower floor our actions. He cautions us that we may observe all the externals of Shabbat yet spend the day thinking and speaking about issues or matters that are totally out of sync with the essence of what Shabbat is.

He concludes that the two levels of Shabbat rest are only experienced when each Jew's actions, words and thoughts ALL reflect the peace, the joy and the calm of this holy day, Shabbat.

In Tune with Torah: elevating our observance of Shabbat to include directing all our thoughts, all our words, as well as all our actions towards deepening our relationship with Hashem.

Personal Thoughts

Lech Lecha

Beresheit/Genesis 12:1 – 17:27

There is so much to capture our attention in this Torah portion that it's a challenge to focus in on just one aspect. However, my attention this week was drawn to this: that for the first time Avraham is referred to as "Avraham the Hebrew (Ivri)" in Beresheit 14:13.

The root of the Hebrew word 'ivri' literally means 'to cross over' and therefore many commentators opine that he is so called at this time because to enter into Israel, he crossed the Euphrates, a major geographical demarcation line in the ancient world. In a more spiritual sense, however, we could also consider that he is called the 'ivri' because in contrast to the rest of the world of his time, Avraham was the only one who 'crossed over' into belief in One True G-d, as opposed to the worship of many gods. He stood alone against the accepted thought of his generation.

A few have suggested that Avraham's decision to embrace monotheism and leave the rest of the world behind, so to speak, indicates his disregard for his fellow man. This is the furthest thing from the truth. When Avraham was commanded by Hashem to leave his land, his birthplace and his father's house, he was promised that *"in you will all the families of the earth be blessed."* (12:4) According to Hashem's promise, Avraham's very separateness will actually become the source of blessing for the entire world.

This reminds us of Isaiah's definition of the national Jewish mission -- to be 'a light unto the nations' (Isaiah 42:6) Avraham 'crossed over' from polytheism to monotheism believing that eventually the rest of the world would join him. While much of the world has indeed accepted monotheism and rejected idol worship, there will yet come a time when all the peoples of the earth will join Avraham in serving the One True G-d in unity of faith and purpose. It is then that Hashem's promise to Avraham will be ultimately fulfilled.

Later in Jewish history, the children of Israel cross the Red Sea in order to escape the Egyptians who are pursuing them. Forty years later, they cross the Jordan to enter into the Promised Land. In both of these events, Avraham's descendants, like their forefather, could only attain to new material and spiritual levels after 'crossing over' a physical border.

In truth, Avraham's experience is a prototype for all of us. Growth in holiness can be described as a series of "crossing over" from a self-centered way of life into a G-d centered way of life. Each 'crossing over' is a decision we make to choose to follow Hashem's ways instead of our own. The sense of 'crossing over' conveys the understanding that we are in fact able to overcome all obstacles in our process of spiritual maturity. As Hashem said to Cain in the parsha of two weeks ago, "sin crouches at the door....but you can overcome it..."

This is the message of Avraham "the Ivri" - all his children have the ability, as he did, to "cross over" from old behaviors to new ones, from worldy ways of thinking to the Torah way of thinking, from selfishness to selflessness. Our ability to do so is our inheritance from our father Avraham.

In Tune with Torah: having the courage and determination to 'cross over' in my own life in any area where change is needed, whether in thought, word or deed.

Personal Thoughts

Vay'era

Bersheit/Genesis 18:1 – 22:24

In this parsha, we read the very first recorded prayer in the Torah, that of Avraham interceding with Hashem for the wicked people of Sodom.

The city was large and prosperous but its people were violent, vile and evil. Immorality of every sort abounded, and in direct opposition to everything that Avraham represented, they were unbelievably cruel towards strangers who happened to pass by their city. Hospitality for them was not a virtue; they were adamantly opposed to showing any kindness whatsoever to anyone who was not a Sodomite.

It was in this atmosphere that Lot, Avraham's nephew, lived. Some time earlier, you may remember, the herdsmen of Lot and the herdsmen of Avraham had some struggles as both men had large flocks and there was not enough grazing land where they lived together for both. Conflicts and tensions arose and Avraham, unwilling to allow strife to continue, gave Lot the opportunity to choose whichever portion of land he wanted for his flocks. Lot chose the territory which included Sodom and Gomorrah because it "looked so good" to him as a place where he could prosper financially. We read no word of consideration for his uncle, Avraham.

Notably, Lot did not say in response to his uncle's offer, "You are the elder and you have been so kind to me. I wouldn't think of choosing first. You choose, Uncle, and I will go in a different direction." No, Lot cared first about Lot.

Living in a debauched society took its toll on Lot as we know from his actions. Yet, when Hashem informed Avraham of His intent to destroy Sodom, Avraham began to intercede.

"Will You destroy the righteous with the wicked?" Avraham petitions. *"If you can find fifty righteous in the city, will you save it for their sake?"* He petitions Hashem repeatedly until he asks if G-d will spare the city of many thousands even for the sake of only ten righteous people in their midst. Hashem says He will.

In the end it becomes obvious that in that wicked city, there were not even ten who were righteous for the city is destroyed, never to be rebuilt.

But what arrests our attention is this: What does Avraham do when he sees that his prayers were essentially rejected? The Torah says that "Avraham remained in his place before Hashem". Despite the apparent failure of his intercession, Avraham remained "in his place" and continued to pray. And though it seems on the surface that his prayers were unanswered, they not only helped save his nephew, Lot, but provided a link to the future Messiah of Israel who is descended from Lot through Ruth, the Moabite.

Furthermore, in his first recorded prayer, Avraham models for every future generation what prayer means to us as individuals and as Jews. Avraham implanted in the Jewish people the realization of the supreme importance of praying for others, even when their 'redemption' or 'deliverance' appears to be so far away and virtually impossible to envision.

Avraham believed that no one was beyond redemption and nothing was so broken that it could not be repaired. Avraham understood that we are put on this earth for Divine purpose; that we are each responsible not just for ourselves but for others; that truly "no man is an island".

Prayer is the greatest gift we give to each other. And prayer that continues when it appears as though our prayers are not being heard is the evidence of the kind of faith Avraham modeled for all of his descendants in every generation.

In Tune with Torah: re-connecting with the truth of the power of prayer and renewing in ourselves dedication to faithfully interceding for those we love and indeed for ALL of Am Yisrael, regardless of how things look externally.

Personal Thoughts

Chayei Sarah

Beresheit/Genesis 23:1 – 25:18

Our Torah portion opens with the death of Sarah and her burial in the Cave of Machpela in the city of Hebron. Why, then, does the Torah portion begin with the words, 'The lifetime of Sarah...'?

The Sages remind us that our "lifetime" is not restricted to the years we spend on this earth, even if they be as long as Sarah's years - 127. The real truth is that our 'lifetime' is two-fold: the years we spend on earth and the life we will enjoy in Olam Haba, the World to Come. Death is not the end; it is a transition of our lifetime to a new form and experience of LIFE.

Therefore, the Torah introduces the event of the death of Sarah with the words, 'The lifetime of Sarah'.

This should remind us of the dictum in Pirkei Avot (The Ethics of the Fathers) which says "This world is like a lobby for the world to come. Prepare yourself in the lobby that you may enter the Banquet Hall."

Every day is precious; every act important, even those we may deem insignificant, for every moment of our earthly life we are preparing ourselves for the world to come.

In the classic work, **Mesilat Yesharim** (The Path of the Just) by the great Sage, Rabbi Moshe Chaim Luzzato, we read, *"A person was not created for his position in this world, but rather for his position in the world-to-come. However, through his position in this world, he acquires his place in the world to come."*

This is not to say that we should be doing good deeds just for the sake of reward -- not at all. Maturity and integrity demand that we do what is right because it is right - and because we honor Hashem by keeping His Torah. It is up to Him to keep accounts. But at the same time, knowing that everything we do matters to Hashem should motivate us in our daily life.

Sarah was buried in Hebron and that also has a message for us. The Cave of Machpela has two chambers, an upper one and a lower one, providing us with a visual picture of what we have just discussed - a lower world and an upper world. From the root of the word, Hebron, comes another word, 'to connect". That Sarah's burial place is in Hebron further reinforces the principle that the lower world and the upper world are connected and that reality is meant to impact our daily life in the here and now.

In Tune with Torah: re-connecting with the truth that our earthly life has a purpose far beyond what we can see with our natural eye; we are here for divine purpose and everything we do really does matter. Taking hold of this truth will have a deep impact on our day to day choices and decisions.

Personal Thoughts

Toldot

Beresheit/Genesis 25:19 – 28:9

It seems that our Patriarchs, the Founding Fathers of Judaism, were enthralled with wellsprings.

First, the Bible tells us of Abraham's involvement in well-digging and his rebuke to the king of the Philistines for allowing his servants to seize one of his wells. Abraham went so far as to perform an elaborate ceremony with the king, during which the king swore that the well would remain in Abraham's possession.

After the death of Abraham, Isaac engages in relentless digging to uncover his father's well which had been stopped up by the Philistines. In addition, we read of at least another four wells that Isaac's servants dug anew. We are even told the names Isaac granted his wells and of the battles he fought to hold on to them!

Jacob, too, seems to harbor special sentiments towards wells. When the Torah describes in next week's portion his journey from Israel to the East, it tells us that *"Jacob looked and behold, a well in the field!"* Jacob spends a lot of time at the well, and it is there that he encounters and decides to marry his wife-to-be, Rachel.

Why were the fathers of the Jewish people so connected to wells? And why does the Torah, a book of instruction and teachings, dedicate a significant part of this week's portion, Toldot, to discuss the details of Isaac's struggles to discover wellsprings?

The two sources of physical waters in our world parallel the two sources of wisdom and spiritual inspiration in our lives.

The first of these spiritual sources, alluding to the rains that fall from the heavens, is a sense of wisdom and inspiration that is born above and beyond the dirt of life's daily challenges. It comes to lucid people at lucid moments; it is straightforward, easy and smooth. These are the waters that emerge from the hearts of pristine spiritual individuals; men and women unsoiled by the filth and muck innate to many a human character. Their waters are delightful and unmuddied.

But then there is the wisdom that emerges from life's "dirt" and grime, from amid much struggle and inner strife; there is the inspiration born from those human hearts that are submerged in the psychological and emotional gravel of life. When a person, burdened by the daily pressures of earning a livelihood and raising a family, and bogged down by his earthly nature and his immoral urges bursts out with a yearning to transcend his dirt and connect to G-d - this small, restricted flow of water seeping out from a sandy and rocky psyche is more refreshing and potent than all of the serene waters located above the "ground".

In Tune with Torah: The fathers of the Jewish people taught us to fight for and to cherish those moments of truth, fleeting as they are, and those small sparks of idealism, transient as they seem, buried within the deep rubble of life's grime and grit.

Those are often the signature moments of life!

Personal Thoughts

Vayetzi

Beresheit/Genesis 28:10 – 32:3

As this Torah portion opens, Yaacov leaves Beer Sheva for Charan where his mother's brother lives. His parents have sent him there to seek a wife from among his own people.

Early in his travels, he reaches what the Torah calls "the place" and lays down to sleep. During the night Hashem gives him a dream which is highly significant and important to Yaacov and indeed to all his descendants to this very day. We commonly refer to this event as "Yaacov's Ladder".

Dreams have been the subject of extensive psychological research and long before modern psychology delved into this subject, the Sages of old cautioned us to pay attention to our dreams as they very often carry a message from heaven.

We know that in the Torah several dreams are pivotal to the unfolding of Jewish history. In a couple of weeks we will be studying Yosef and his dreams which are no less important than the one we meditate on this Shabbat.

What multiple insights can we gain from Yaacov's dream of a ladder planted firmly in the earth and reaching to the heavens with angels ascending and descending upon it? Keeping in mind that entire books have been written about the implications of this dream, we will look at just a fraction of its significance.

The dream is symbolic of Israel's future and the Sages note the following various insights that support this thesis.

First of all, it alludes to the giving of the Torah at Sinai where Moshe and Aharon ascended and descended Mt. Sinai. Interestingly, the gematria (numerical value) of the word ladder -- 'sulam' is exactly the same as the gematria for 'Sinai' -- the value of both words is 130.

The ladder also alludes to the altar in the Temple which would be built in the future. The altar stood on the ground but the fragrance of its sacrifices ascended to the heavens and the angels are symbolic of the cohanim (priests) who ascended to the altar to offer the sacrifices and then descended afterwards.

Thirdly the dream foretells the exile of the Jewish people and the destruction of the Temple. In Daniel

3 we read that Nebuchadnezzar, who took the Jews into exile, built a very tall idol. In Hebrew the word 'ladder' as we saw above is 'sulam' and the very same Hebrew letters transposed form the word 'semel' which is 'idol' or 'statue'.

The Midrash says that Yaacov saw the guardian angels of the great empires -- Babylon, Persia, Greece and Rome -- ascend the rungs of the ladder in turn and then fall to the ground. The angel over Babylon climbed 70 steps and fell - the angel of Persia climbed 52 steps and fell, the angel of Greece climbed 180 rungs and fell and lastly the angel of Edom (Rome) climbed so high that Yaacov became frighted that Edom would reach the Throne of Glory. Hashem answered Yaacov by saying that Edom (Rome) will climb almost to the heavens but will ultimately fall for only Israel -- in the end -- will climb all the way to Hashem's Throne of Glory and not fall back.

Finally, an additional meaning brought forth is that the world is like a ladder; the cycles of the history of nations and peoples is one of ascending and descending. Nations and empires rise and fall.

So do people.

Each of us has 'highs' and 'lows' in life yet through it all, just as He did with Yaacov, "Hashem stands over us" to be with us and keep us through all of life's expected and unexpected events.

In Tune with Torah: let us consider our own dreams in light of this one given to our forefather, Yaacov and ask Hashem to illuminate our minds to perceive whatever messages He communicates to us through the dreams we may have had in the past or may have in the future.

Personal Thoughts

Vayishlach

Beresheit/Genesis 32:4 – 36:43

Rarely, if at all, do we perceive when a specific moment or event in our life contains within it such a depth of effect that generations of our descendants are qualitatively affected because of that one single experience of ours. This is exactly what we have in this week's Torah portion.

We read in Beresheit/Genesis 32 that the patriarch, Yaacov, is returning to the Land of Israel with his wives and children and on the way will encounter his brother, Esav, who is approaching him with 400 men. Yaacov is very frightened for he well remembers that some 20 years earlier, Esav had determined to kill him.

He therefore prepares a generous gift from his own wealth and dispatches messengers to deliver it to Esav.

He prays to Hashem for deliverance from his brother's evil intent towards him and takes practical action to protect his family. He divides his large entourage into two camps thinking that if Esav attacks one at least the other will be safe.

After settling his family in the two camps, we read that *"Yaacov was left alone...and he wrestled with a man throughout the long night until the break of dawn....."*

What is the message here?

In fact, there are several.

It was night and Yaacov is completely alone in the dark. Without a doubt, he is wrestling within himself, symbolic of every man's inner struggle between good and evil. But there is much more to it than that.

Wrestling all night is a vivid prophetic picture of the future of Yaacov's descendants to the present day. "Night" represents the centuries of Jewish history that will pass before the glorious day of the arrival of the Mashiach, alluded to as 'the break of dawn.'

The very essence of Israel is to continue to struggle 'all night' -- to wrestle with its own calling, to stand fast in the face of opposition and to believe without wavering in the promises of the Covenant made by Hashem with Avraham. Indeed, one of the thirteen articles of faith penned by Maimonides is this: *"I believe with complete faith in the coming of*

Mashiach; even though he tarry, nevertheless, I yearn every day for his coming."

The Midrash identifies Yaacov's opponent as Esav's angel who when he perceived he could not overcome Yaacov, struck his side and dislocated Yaacov's hip.

If you have ever known someone who suffered a broken hip, or a dislocated hip, you already know that this condition is extremely debilitating. The hips support the upper body. Generally a broken or dislocated hip renders the person unable to stand, much less to continue to wrestle -- which is exactly what Yaacov did!

Our Patriarch continued the struggle until dawn, demonstrating to us that when daybreak comes, the power of the opponent is broken. When the dawn of Mashiach's appearance arrives, every opponent of Israel will be rendered powerless.

And not only that...When Esav's angel saw that he was unable to vanquish Yaacov, he said, 'Let me go for the dawn is breaking.' But Yaacov responded, 'I will not let you go until you bless me.'

It was not enough just to prevail. Yaacov wanted his opponent's blessing.

And what is the blessing Esav's angel gives to Yaacov? Freely translated, the angel says, 'You are Yaacov no more; you are Israel because you struggled with G-d and man and you have prevailed.'

The day will come when all the nations who have refused to recognize and affirm Israel's divine mission, who resented Israel's birthright and blessing, will themselves finally bless Israel and submit to its leadership. The prophet Isaiah spoke of it eloquently:

"Thus says the L-rd G-d, 'I will lift up My hand to the nations and raise My banner to the peoples and they shall bring your sons in their arms and carry your daughters on their backs. Kings shall tend to your children and their queens shall serve you as nurses. They shall bow down to you [Israel], face to the ground, and lick the dust of your feet and you shall know that I am Hashem. Those who trust in Me shall not be ashamed.' " Isaiah 49:22-23

After long years of enmity between the brothers, reconciliation occurs between Yaacov and Esav, but only after Yaacov wrestles and suffers the dislocation of his hip. From that day on, he limps and the Sages suggest that his limp is a sign of the pain Israel carries when some of its children turn away from walking with Hashem because of the struggle involved in seeking a life of holiness.

In Tune with Torah: Each of us needs to come to terms with the reality that wrestling is a normal, even desirable part of life for it is in our 'wrestling' that we are changed -- as was Yaacov -- from being known as a 'supplanter' to becoming Israel, a prince of G-d.

Personal Thoughts

Vayeishev

Beresheit/Genesis 37:1 – 40:23

There is a passage in the Talmud that says "the actions of the fathers are a sign to the children." (Sotah 34a) This concept is deeply embedded in the Torah and in Jewish thinking, and in this portion of Vayeishev, a vivid example of it is portrayed.

One of Judaism's cornerstones is a firm belief in the power of *teshuva*, sincere repentance. The event in Judah's life which we will now review provides a paradigm for repentance and how appropriate that the Hebrew word, *teshuva*, and the Hebrew title of this portion, *vayeishev,* both have a common root, *shev*, which means "to return".

After Yosef was sold into slavery on Judah's advice, his brothers blamed him. His response was to separate himself from them in a kind of voluntary exile. *"And it came to pass at that time that Judah went away from his brothers."* 38:1

During this prolonged period, Judah married and his wife gave birth to three sons. Years passed and his firstborn married a young woman named Tamar, but he died for the sin of spilling his seed. Tamar then married her husband's brother, Judah's second son according to the tradition of levirate marriage, but he was no different than his older brother. Instead of impregnating his wife, he also spilled his seed and was punished with an early death.

One son was left and Judah, no doubt distraught at the loss of his two older sons, promised Tamar his last son but did not deliver on his promise for a long time.

Tamar, whom historical sources say was a virtuous and holy woman, had an inner prophetic sense that she was somehow destined to have children of the family of Judah whose descendants would be royalty and key figures in the unfolding of the history of the people of Israel. The longer she waited for Judah to arrange her marriage with his third son, the more she became convinced that he would fail to do so. Tamar decided it was time for action.

She disguised herself as a roadside harlot and enticed her father-in-law to sleep with her, not recognizing who she was. Wisely, she requested and received personal items belonging to Judah as assurance of payment to follow.

Shortly thereafter, learning that his widowed daughter-in-law was pregnant, Judah was incensed and condemned her to death.

Tamar's response to his edict was to send back to Judah the personal items he had left with her, proving to him the identity of the man who had impregnated her.

At this pivotal moment, Judah was faced with a choice. Either he could say nothing and she would be killed, or he could honestly admit his failure and accept responsibility for his actions.

Judah made the right choice and publicly proclaimed, as recorded in the Torah, *"She is more righteous than I."* 38:26 He repented for not doing his duty by giving his third son to her as a husband and the Torah testifies that *"he did not know her [intimately] further."* 38:27

There are three steps to true repentance: acknowledgement of the wrongdoing, sincere remorse for the sin, and when faced with the opportunity to repeat it, choosing instead to do right.

Judah fulfilled all three of these steps and thereby became a model of true repentance for every generation. "The actions of the fathers are [indeed] a sign to the children."

The idea that Hashem is involved in even difficult predicaments such as this one can be derived from Judah's confession: "She is more righteous than I."

Rashi explains that no harm is done to the integrity of the text by splitting the statement in two: "She is more righteous - it is from me."

In this view, the latter part of the statement can have a two fold meaning. On the one hand, Judah could be understood to be saying, "it [the pregnancy] is from me." On the other hand, Hashem Himself could be understood to say that "It is from Me [that this whole situation happened, to assure that the future kings of Israel would descend from Judah.]

Put in the context of what was happening 'at that time' (38:1), this is an interesting possibility. For 'at that time', the brothers were busy selling Yosef; Yosef, Ya'acov and Reuven were all in mourning because of the events surrounding Yosef's disappearance; Yehudah (Judah) was busy finding a wife; and Hashem – at the very same time – was busy preparing the light of the Mashiach!

In other words, the actions of all concerned were, in a mysterious way known and understood only by Hashem, paving the way for the key descendants of the House of Judah, King David and much later, David's royal descendant, the Mashiach Himself.

We see a similarly mysterious unfolding of events in the time of Esther, an account which also includes specific events that are perplexing. Yet Hashem was in the background, orchestrating it all for Israel's ultimate good and for the fulfillment of His eternal plan.

In Tune with Torah: it is a healthy exercise to look back over our lives and reflect on events and situations which at the time were difficult, incomprehensible and even traumatic, and with the benefit of hindsight, to indentify the hand of Hashem guiding us, even in the darkness.

Personal Thoughts

Miketz

Beresheit/Genesis 41:1 – 44:17

The story of Joseph continues with the words, *"It was two years to the day..."*

Such a specific explanation of time has a reason. The Sages say that it is to teach us that there is no suffering that lasts forever. Joseph's 12 years in prison were coming to an end, even as it is written in Job 28:3 *"He sets an end to darkness..."*

Immediately following this opening statement, we read of Pharaoh's two dreams and his frustration when his own seers could not interpret them. It is at this point that the Cupbearer remembers Joseph in prison and tells Pharaoh about him.

Joseph is rushed from the prison to appear before the ruler of Egypt and upon hearing Pharaoh's dreams, explains their message and advises Pharaoh on how to prepare for the coming calamity.

It is interesting to note that dreams (Joseph's own) brought about his humiliation and now dreams (Pharaoh's) bring about his exaltation.

On appointing Joseph as ruler of Egypt, second only to himself, Pharaoh gives Joseph a new name,

Zaphenath Paneah which means "the revealer of that which is hidden..."

Joseph had indeed himself been hidden in slavery and then in prison yet within him was the 'light' which Pharaoh would need at the appropriate time to save not just the Egyptians but Jacob and his descendants as well.

He was hidden in order to be revealed at the right time.

Is it any wonder that the story of Joseph is read each year around the time of Hanukkah? There is a deep connection between the two.

When the Greeks had destroyed the Temple but the Macabbees prevailed over them, one small vial of pure oil was found in the rubble - hidden to be revealed at just the right time. There was only enough oil for one day yet miraculously, the Menorah burned for eight days.

In Hebrew, the word, 'chinuch', which means 'education' shares the same root as the word Hanukkah which tells us that Hanukkah is meant to educate, both Jews and non-Jews.

To the Jew, Hanukkah is a powerful reminder of our calling as a people: to be a LIGHT TO THE NATIONS.

To the non-Jew, Hanukkah testifies that though we suffer persecution, destruction, and exile, there will always be, as it were, at least one 'vial of oil' of Judaism left hidden among the nations to preserve the covenant which Hashem made with Avraham, Yitzhak and Ya'acov.

This is why Hanukkah is the only Jewish holiday which we are commanded to celebrate publicly. The eight branch menorah, called a Hanukkiah, is to be placed in a window or just outside the front door of the home so its lights can be seen by everyone.

During the course of Hanukkah we light a total of 36 candles, each one a reminder that within every Jew is the spark of a tzaddik (a holy, righteous person) as Isaiah 60:21 declares 'all Your people are tzaddikim...'

If Israel is going to fulfill her calling to be a light to the nations, how can our observance of Hanukkah help us achieve that goal?

The lighting of the candles each night has a profound meaning, far deeper than just preserving the memory of a great miracle. I suggest that the eight candles represent individually the following concepts: knowledge, understanding, wisdom, righteous fear of G-d, love for G-d, love for the Torah, love for the Land of Israel and love towards our fellow Jews.

On the first night, we pray as we light the candle that our knowledge of G-d would increase; the second night, our understanding of His ways; the third night, for wisdom and so on.

By the last day of Hanukkah, as we have focused on these eight qualities needed in every Jewish soul, we begin to see the vision emerge of how Israel can truly be a "Light to the Nations". As each individual Jew, represented by the individual candles of the hanukkiah, grows in knowledge, understanding and wisdom, in righteous fear of heaven, love of G-d and His Torah, love of Israel and all her people, the entire nation is elevated closer and closer to its mission of being a holy people unto Hashem and through that holiness spreading His light throughout the world.

Joseph, the 'revealer of that which is hidden, typifies all of Am Yisrael, hidden among the nations, but ONLY hidden, like the flask of oil for the PURPOSE of being revealed at the right time.

In Tune with Torah: May Israel's mission come forth and be fulfilled, even in our day and may it begin with me. In what area of my life do I need more 'light'? Is there 'light' that I am ignoring?

Personal Thoughts

Vayigash

Beresheit/Genesis 44:18 – 47:27

There are rare and unique moments in world history that men or nations remember and one such moment occurs in this week's Torah portion. We read the deeply moving account of Joseph revealing himself to his brothers who are stunned to the core.

As they stand there speechless, he says to them: *"I am your brother Joseph, whom you sold into Egypt! And now, do not be distressed and do not be angry with yourselves for selling me here, because it was to save lives that God sent me ahead of you. For two years now there has been famine in the land, and for the next five years there will be no plowing and reaping. But God sent me ahead of you to preserve for you a remnant on earth and to save your lives by a great deliverance. So then, it was not you who sent me here, but God."* (Gen. 45: 4-8)

This is the first recorded moment in history in which one human being forgives another.

This is a very big deal!!!

Joseph forgives. That is a first in history. There is even a hint in the Torah of the newness of this event. Many years later, after their father Jacob has died, the brothers come to Joseph fearing that he will now take revenge. They concoct a story:

They sent word to Joseph, saying, "Your father left these instructions before he died: 'This is what you are to say to Joseph: I ask you to forgive your brothers for the sins and the wrongs they committed in treating you so badly.' Now please forgive the sins of the servants of the God of your father." When their message came to him, Joseph wept. [Gen. 50: 16-18]

The brothers understand the word "forgive" – this is the first time it appears explicitly in the Torah – but they are still unsure about it. Did Joseph really mean it the first time? Can someone really forgive those who sold him into slavery?

Joseph weeps that his brothers haven't really understood that he meant it when he said it.

But he did, then and now.

There is nothing accidental about Joseph's behavior. In fact from the moment the brothers appear before him in Egypt for the first time to the moment when he announces his identity and forgives them, there is an immensely detailed account of the process of earning forgiveness.

First he accuses them of a crime they have not committed. He says they are spies. He has them imprisoned for three days. Then, holding Shimon as a hostage, he tells them that they must now go back home and bring back their youngest brother Benjamin. In other words, he is forcing them to re-enact that earlier occasion when they came back to their father with one of the brothers, Joseph, missing. Look at what happens next:

They said to one another, "Surely we deserve to be punished because of our brother. We saw how distressed he was when he pleaded with us for his life, but we would not listen; that's why this distress has come on us" ... They did not realize that Joseph could understand them, since he was using an interpreter. [Gen. 42: 21-23]

Here is the first stage of repentance. **They admit they have done wrong.**

Next, after the second meeting, Joseph has his special silver cup planted in Benjamin's sack. It is found and the brothers are brought back. They are told that Benjamin must stay as a slave.

"What can we say to my lord?" Judah replied. *"What can we say? How can we prove our innocence? God has uncovered your servants' guilt. We are now my lord's slaves—we ourselves and the one who was found to have the cup."* [Gen. 44: 16]

Here is the second stage of repentance. **They confess.** They do more: they admit collective responsibility. This is important. When the brothers sold Joseph into slavery it was Judah who proposed the crime (37: 26-27) but they were all (except Reuben) complicit in it.

Finally, at the climax of the story Judah himself says *"So now let me remain as your slave in place of the lad. Let the lad go back with his brothers!"* (42: 33). Judah, who sold Joseph as a slave, is now willing to become a slave so that his brother Benjamin can go free.

As we explained in the portion of Vayeishev, this is what the sages and Maimonides define as **complete repentance**, namely when circumstances repeat themselves and you have an opportunity to commit the same crime again, but you refrain from doing so because you have changed.

Now Joseph can forgive, because his brothers, led by Judah, have gone through all three stages of repentance: [1] admission of guilt, [2] confession and [3] behavioral change.

Forgiveness only exists in a culture in which repentance exists. Repentance presupposes that we are free and morally responsible agents who are capable of change, specifically the change that comes about when we recognize that something we have done is wrong and we are responsible for it and we must never do it again.

Forgiveness is not just one idea among many. It transformed the human situation. For the first time it established the possibility that we are not condemned endlessly to repeat the past. When I repent I show that I can change. And when I forgive I show that my action is not mere reaction, the way revenge would be. Forgiveness breaks the irreversibility of the past, the undoing of what was done.

Humanity changed the day Joseph forgave his brothers. When we forgive and are worthy of being forgiven, we are no longer prisoners of our past.

In Tune with Torah: checking our own relationships to be sure that we have fully forgiven others and that we ourselves have sought forgiveness from whomever it is needed.

Personal Thoughts

Vayechi

Beresheit/Genesis 47:28 – 50:26

Near the end of this Torah portion, we read: *"When Joseph's brothers saw that their father was dead, they said, 'What if Joseph still bears a grudge against us and pays us back for all the wrong we did to him!' So they sent this message to Joseph: 'Before his death your father left this instruction: So shall you say to Joseph, Forgive, I urge you, the offense and guilt of your brothers who treated you so harshly. Therefore, please forgive the offense of the servants of the G-d of your father.' And Joseph was in tears when they spoke to him."*

After being with Joseph for 17 years in Egypt and after seeing all the good that he did for them, as well as his declaration earlier that he understood that it was not they who sent him to Egypt, but G-d in order that many lives be preserved, why at this late date do we find his brothers still harboring the fear that he would avenge their treatment of him so many years earlier?

One might suggest that the death of their father re-awakened their fears for they may have thought that his kindness towards them was only because of his father's presence but now that he was dead, he would feel free to retaliate for their betrayal.

I think it goes deeper than that.

When he revealed himself to them 17 years earlier, he had assured them, as we said above, that he recognized the hand of Divine Providence in sending him to Egypt and therefore, he held no bitter feelings toward them. He embraced them at that time, he showered them with gifts, he made provision for them to live peacefully and happily in Goshen, they and their families and their flocks.

Then, why now, after so many years, do they question his attitude?

Could it be because they have not yet forgiven themselves?

There is a principle in psychology called the 'mirror syndrome' which explains that human beings often attribute to others the weaknesses within themselves. When coupled with the inability to forgive oneself for previous errors or wrongdoings, it leads to behavior exactly like this that we are discussing.

The brothers still felt very guilty for having betrayed him and his forgiveness and kindness toward them reinforced their guilt precisely because they had not yet forgiven themselves. Therefore they assumed -- because of their own guilt -- that Joseph would still be looking for an opportunity to get even.

Apparently there was still within them a tendency towards taking one's own revenge for that is what they attributed to their brother. Without understanding the true nature of forgiveness, this is how human beings think.

When Joseph received their message, he wept, for he realized that they had not truly believed him when he forgave them and surely, they had yet to forgive themselves and let go of the past. It is noteworthy that he did not get angry; rather he was very sad.

He responded: *"Have no fear! Am I a substitute for G-d? Besides, although you intended to do me harm, G-d intended it for good, so as to bring about the present result - the salvation of many people. And so, fear not, I will sustain you and your children."* Thus he reassured them, speaking kindly to them.

As painful as it may be for any of us when we are hurt or betrayed by someone we love, it is even MORE painful if they do not or cannot accept our forgiveness towards them. At that point, we have a choice - anger or kindness. It is incumbent upon us to choose the path of Joseph -- to show kindness and reassurance which is the greatest means of helping the one who offended us to forgive themselves.

In Tune with Torah: ask yourself whether or not you are harboring any guilt over errors or offenses that have been forgiven in the past by G-d and/or by others. If you are, resolve to forgive yourself -- NOW -- and let it go.

And if someone you know has difficulty accepting your forgiveness, do not be angry but with kindness, understand their struggle and do what you can to help them forgive themselves.

Personal Thoughts

Shemot/Exodus

The Second Book
Of the Torah

Shemot
Shemot/Exodus 1:1 – 6:1

We now begin reading the second book of the Torah, Shemot which in the English Bibles is entitled "Exodus". However, the Hebrew word "Shemot" literally means 'names' and it is highly significant that this is the name given to this book in its original language because the issue of 'names' is very important throughout this book.

On a basic level, we know that each book of the Torah is named from one of the first words in the first verse of the respective book. Shemot begins with *"And these are the names of those who went down to Egypt with Ya'acov..."*

What are some of the other reasons why this book is called Shemot?

First of all, it was in Egypt that Ya'acov's family became a nation and his personal name given to him by Hashem, Israel, became the name of the nation and remains so to this day.

Secondly, it is in this book that Hashem for the first time reveals His ineffable Name - the four letter Yud-Hey-Vav-Hey - to Israel and indeed to the gentile nations. Up until this time He had revealed

Himself to the Patriarchs and other early figures in biblical history only in part by names that referred more to some of His characteristics and His works than His very Essence. But in Shemot He reveals to Moshe and to the children of Israel His most holy Name, the Name that plumbs the depths of His very Essence.

However, as we will see later this Name is also revealed to the Pharaoh when Moshe confronts the Egyptian leader with the demand, *"Let My people go..."* Pharaoh responds *"Who is this G-d..."* And in the continuing saga of the various confrontations between Moshe and the Pharaoh, it becomes abundantly clear, especially through the plagues, that Pharaoh comes to a recognition that there is indeed One True G-d and that He is the G-d of the Hebrews.

Traditionally, Jewish people do not pronounce the Four Letter Name of G-d out of an awesome respect for its profound holiness since it denotes the very essence of G-d Himself. The English translation of "I will be who I will be" falls far short of the depth conveyed in the original Hebrew letters which form this name. (For more study on this topic, I recommend the book "The Hebrew Letters" by Rabbi Yitzhak Ginsberg.

The plagues were designed not only to convince Pharaoh to let the Israelites go but also to teach the children of Israel WHO their G-d was and to nurture their faith in Him. Hashem wanted them to fully understand that their approaching deliverance was His doing and His alone -- it was not to be wrought by human means. They were to know without a doubt -- and teach their children for generations to come -- that they were delivered from slavery in Egypt by the very hand of their Creator and King.

In the third chapter of Shemot, Hashem says to Moshe, *"I am the G-d of your father, the G-d of Avraham, the G-d of Yitzhak and the G-d of Yaacov. This is my Name forever...."*

Interestingly, in the Hebrew text of this verse, the word 'olam' (which means forever) is written without the letter 'vav' which allows an alternative translation: "This is my Name to be concealed..." alluding to a profound principle which is seen in all creation.

Hashem is at the same time revealed AND concealed. He is revealed as the Creator to those who have eyes to see the world as His handiwork, but nature also conceals Him, for we see His work but not He, Himself.

He is revealed in the life of a godly, saintly person yet is also at the same time concealed for we see the individual who reflects His likeness but we do not see Him!

Likewise, His essential Name reveals a depth of His essence but also conceals it for who of us can truly plumb the deepest depths of what it means to be "I AM who I AM..."

We can also learn from this that our own personal names are important. When Jewish parents name their children, they ask themselves several questions: What is the meaning of this name? What does it connote about the path in life that this child is destined to take? What do I desire for this new child?

Hebrew names have very profound meanings as witnessed when Hashem changed Avram's name to Avraham, Sarai's name to Sarah, Ya'acov's name to Israel. Each change directly impacted their mission in life.

Even if your parents chose your name for apparently simpler reasons, if you seek it, you will surely find a message, a meaning, a significance to your name. It may be a positive influence; it may have some negative conotation which is why at times, people change their names.

In Tune with Torah: taking some time to meditate on why Hashem would say "This is my name forever - the G-d of Avraham, the G-d of Yitzhak and the G-d of Ya'acov..." What is it about that particular name of His that Hashem showed such a special affinity for it?

And furthermore, ponder what message may He want to give each of us about our own names and their connection to our personal mission in life?

Personal Thoughts

Va'eira

Shemot/Exodus 6:2 – 9:35

The Biblical account of the Jewish Exodus from Egypt has been one of the most inspiring stories for the oppressed, enslaved and downtrodden throughout history. The narrative of the Exodus has provided countless peoples with the courage to hope for a better future, and to act on their dream.

After Moses' first visit to Pharaoh demanding 'Let My people go' the Egyptian monarch increased their torture. The Hebrews didn't want to hear anything more about the promise of redemption. Now look with me at the next verse, a seemingly strange verse in this weekly portion.

So G-d spoke to Moses and to Aaron, and He commanded them to the children of Israel, and to Pharaoh the king of Egypt, to let the children of Israel out of the land of Egypt.

G-d is charging Moses with two directives: Command the people of Israel and then command Pharaoh the king. The message for Pharaoh is clear: Let the children of Israel out of Egypt. But what is it that Moses is supposed to command the people themselves?

The answer to this question is profoundly simple and moving, and is vital to the understanding of freedom from a Torah perspective.

Before Pharaoh can liberate the Jewish slaves, they, themselves, must be ready to become free. You can take a man out of slavery, but it is an entirely different matter to take the slavery out of a man. Externally, you may be free; internally you may still be enslaved.

What is the first and foremost symptom of being free? That you learn to give freedom to others.

The dictator, the controller, or the abusive spouse or parent, does not know how to give others freedom. He (or she) feels compelled to force others into the mold that he has created for them. Uncomfortable in his own skin, he is afraid that someone will overshadow him, expose his weaknesses, usurp his position or make him feel like an "extra" in this world. He may appear powerful, but inwardly his power is a symptom of his own inner misery and insecurity.

Only when we learn to embrace others, not for who we would like them to be, but for who they truly are, can we begin to embrace ourselves, not for who we wish we were, but for exactly who we are. When we free those around us, we are freeing ourselves. By accepting them, we learn to accept ourselves.

He alone is powerful who empowers others. He alone is free who can free others. He alone is a true leader who creates other leaders.

I believe it was Abraham Lincoln who once said, *"Nearly all men can stand adversity, but if you want to test a man's character, give him power."*

So let us ask ourselves, do we know how to celebrate the soaring success of our loved ones and acquaintances? Do we encourage them to spread their wings and maximize their potentials? Are we able to allow others to shine without feeling ourselves diminished?

Anyone can be set free physically. But former slaves can easily become present tyrants if their release from slavery is only physical and not mental and emotional. If the inner attitudes of the mind and heart don't change, removing the external bondage of slavery does little good. People who were abused often become abusers themselves. It is all they know about life so the cycle goes on.

The first Mitzvah the Jews had to hear from Moses before he could appeal to Pharaoh to let them go was this: Hashem, your G-d, wants Pharaoh to set you free but only you can set yourself free from within. Freedom is a gift from on high, not just for you, but that you should also pass it on to others. You will only be able to do that if you set your own soul free, leaving the past behind and moving on with your whole heart and soul, not just your body.

In Tune with Torah: Resolve to accept your loved ones and friends exactly as they are - right now - and love them without reservation; give your children and grandchildren the "right" to fail if necessary and still know that they are loved. A wise man I knew years ago said something I've never forgotten: to deny a man the right to fall is to deny him the right to grow. May we all grow through our own past mistakes but having learned the lesson, move on to greater and greater maturity in life.

Personal Thoughts

Bo
Shemot/Exodus 10:1 – 13:16

In this Torah portion the final three plagues are recorded and each one of them has something to do with darkness.

The Torah says that the swarm of locusts was so thick that the land was darkened. (10:15) Can you just imagine living through that?

It is interesting to note that this is the first time that Pharaoh's servants rebuke him (10:7). When Moshe and Aaron warn Pharaoh of the coming plague of locusts, Pharaoh's servants appeal to Pharaoh, asking him if does not yet realize that Egypt is being destroyed? They urge him to let the people go, but Pharaoh remains defiant. What he does do, however, is that for the first time he acknowledges that he has sinned but he does NOT show true repentance. For he asks that Moshe *"forgive me just this time..."* (10:16).

True repentance begins with acknowledgement of wrongdoing but follows that with sincere regret and a resolve not to repeat the offense. Pharaoh's acknowledgment is a good start but he fails to follow through with regret and resolve to change his behavior.

The next plague brought thick and palpable darkness throughout the entire land of Egypt. No one could move for three days. Prisoners of war in the last century who were imprisoned in total darkness for days on end testified that they emerged from the darkness totally disoriented and weak. One can only imagine the effect on the entire Egyptian nation during this plague of darkness.

However, in Goshen, where the children of Israel lived, there was light.

The final plague, the Death of the Firstborn, struck at midnight -- in the darkness of night. Before it began, Moshe had carefully passed on to the children of Israel Hashem's precise instructions as to what they were to do before and during the Plague.

First they were to obtain for themselves, each family, a lamb which they were to keep at their home for 4 days. This required faith on their part for the Egyptians worshipped sheep as one of their gods. Should the Egyptians begin to catch on to the plans of the Israelites to slaughter the lamb, the lives of the Hebrews could well have been in danger.

The second test of faith was associated with the commandment to take of the blood of the lamb and brush it on their doorpost and lintel and then to gather the entire family in the house, behind closed doors for when the Angel of Death passed over Egypt, the blood on the doorpost would save the lives of those within the house.

When the plague began, the Israelites would certainly have heard the cries and screams that would be emanating from the Egyptian homes as one after another, the firstborn in each home was discovered to be dead. Fear mixed with curiosity would so easily have aroused in the Israelites the temptation to open the door and look out, or lean out of a window to try to see what was happening. Perhaps the Egyptians were becoming infuriated and gathering to attack the Hebrews in retaliation?

Their salvation depended on total obedience to the word of Hashem as delivered through Moshe - brush some of the blood on the doorpost and lintel and then go in and close the door! Only within the confines that Hashem set for them would they be safe.

These two aspects of the Exodus teach us about the two sides of FAITH. There are times when faith demands action as in the procurement of the lamb and holding it in one's home for 4 days despite the danger it potentially represented. The action prompted by faith was the mitzvah and by doing so, the Hebrews were protected.

There are other times when faith demands that we be still and wait quietly, as when the children of Israel had to remain in their locked homes despite whatever uproar of outpoured grief could be heard in the land. Their 'salvation' in that instance depended not on action, but on quiet trust in Hashem.

One of the challenges of our lives is to learn when our Emuna (faith) needs to be expressed in action and when it is best expressed in quiet waiting upon Hashem. Who of us has not made the mistake of trying to 'take matters into our own hands' instead of waiting for Hashem to handle a certain problem or difficulty? And who of us has not perhaps 'waited' when Hashem was prompting us to act but we were fearful or unwilling to do what He impressed upon us to do?

The process of growing into mature faith is a journey of learning how to recognize Hashem's direction to us and following His leading.

In Tune with Torah: Let us renew our willingness to be lifelong learners in the ways of Emuna. May

Hashem help each of us to recognize His direction more clearly with each passing week; that we may discern accurately when we are to wait for His intervention and when we are to act according to His direction.

Personal Thoughts

Beshalach
Shemot/Exodus 13:17 – 17:16

Parsha Beshalach contains key events in early Jewish history and an abundance of spiritual insights for our inner development and growth.

This portion is usually read on Shabbat Shira (Sabbath of Song) because it is this week that we review the miraculous crossing of the Sea of Reeds by the Children of Israel at the completion of which, the entire congregation explodes into a joyous and thankful song of praise to Hashem for His awesome deliverance.

After the former Hebrew slaves left Egypt, they traveled into the desert, and very soon, Pharaoh regretted his decision to let them go, assembled his army and set out to bring back his slave laborers. When the Israelites saw the Egyptian army approaching in the distance, they were terrified and cried out to Hashem. In response, Hashem's instructions through Moshe were: *"Do not fear! Stand still...and see the salvation of Hashem..."*

He commanded Moshe to raise his staff over the waters, the sea parted and the entire nation crossed over on dry land. The Egyptians, seeing this wonder, plunged in impulsively to pursue their prey and were subsequently drowned as the sea returned to its normal state. Seeing the utter defeat of the Egyptians, the children of Israel broke into exuberant song. Miriam picked up her tambourine and led the women in singing and dancing.

This event teaches us several important lessons.

It is the first record of the nation -- as a nation -- singing to Hashem and brings to our attention the power of music.

You are no doubt aware that every Hebrew letter has a corresponding numerical value and that when two words in Hebrew have the same numerical value, it indicates that there is a deep connection between them. In that light, it is very significant to learn that the Hebrew word for 'song' has a numerical value of 515 and the Hebrew word for 'prayer', tefillah, also has the numerical value of 515, which tells us that prayer and song are profoundly related.

We know that King David sang to the Almighty and indeed, he is described as 'the sweet singer of Israel'. When King Saul was troubled by evil spirits, they would send for David and it is recorded that when David played music for the king, the evil spirits departed from him.

Dvora, the judge, sang a glorious song with Barak after the defeat of the armies of Sisera.

Hannah broke out into passionate song at the birth of the prophet Samuel.

The Psalms are replete with such phrases as *"I will sing unto Hashem for He has triumphed gloriously...",* this verse from Psalm 3 being just one example.

In the 1700's, the Baal Shem Tov grieved over the dry, mechanical form of prayer prevalent in his day in the communities of Europe and he initiated a revolution of joy, passion and music in the worship of Hashem. Words without music, he believed, were like a body without a soul. The effects of his 'revolution' are evident to this day in congregational services that are alive with enthusiastic singing and joy.

But what about our personal times of prayer? Do we find it difficult to concentrate on our prayers? Is praying with 'kavana' a challenge?

I suggest that combining song with our personal, private prayer and meditation can greatly enhance our ability to maintain our focus on Hashem during prayer. In fact, I do more than 'suggest'; I can testify from personal experience that singing our prayers does indeed greatly enhance our ability to remain focused on Hashem during private prayer and I highly endorse the practice.

It is not necessary to have a beautiful voice in order to utilize this aid in prayer. Use the voice Hashem gave you for He listens to the song emanating from your soul. Whatever quality of voice He gave you was His choice for you when you were created - use what He gave you with your whole heart for that is what honors Him. In your relationship to Him as a child to its Father, Hashem delights in your singing to Him as any father delights in the song of his child.

In Tune with Torah: Let us take to heart the exhortation of David, 'sweet singer of Israel', as found in Psalm146: *My soul, praise Hashem; I will praise Hashem with my life; I will sing to Hashem as long as I live...* Sing to Him -- sing for joy and watch your times of prayer become more and more powerful and joyful.

Personal Thoughts

Yitro
Shemot/Exodus 18:1 – 20:23

Three months after the Exodus from Egypt, the Children of Israel arrived at Mt. Sinai. Hashem then spoke to Moshe to tell the children of Israel, *'...you have seen what I did to Egypt, and that I have borne you on the wings of eagles and brought you to Me.'* Why the description 'on wings of eagles'?

The eagle is an amazing creation of Hashem from which Israel was to learn some very valuable lessons -- and so must we today.

1) The Eagle has NO FEAR of its enemy. Regardless of the size of the enemy or the weapon it holds, the eagle attacks forcefully with no concern about itself. Its instinct is to protect what it loves.

2) The Eagle is a tenacious creature. It will actually look for and fly into fierce storms. When smaller creatures run and hide themselves at an approaching storm, the eagle spreads its massive wings and soars above the storm's winds to amazing heights. Eagles actually use the storms to lift themselves up. It is as if they recognize that storms are the tools for greater development. Need I say more?

3) The Eagle is a nurturing creature. One is hard pressed to find any other bird that is as attentive to and gentle with its young. As the baby eaglet grows to a certain stage of development, the mother eagle will carry it on her back, then suddenly swoop out from under it, forcing the eaglet to fly. If the baby eaglet falls instead of flying, the mother will swoop down under it and save it lest it injure itself but will then begin the process again. She will teach and train her young until they learn how to soar to the heights.

4) The Eagle teaches us the great value of a balanced life. It can soar as high as 10,000 ft. but also glide rapidly (up to 75 mph) down to earth to save its young or to obtain food. In other words, the eagle knows when to soar and when to be firmly planted on the earth. It can be comfortable in both areas.

5) The Eagle never eats dead meat. It is not a scavenger like the vulture. The eagle hunts and consumes its own food, urging us by implication to be seekers of Hashem's 'food' -- the Torah. While commentaries and spiritual books are a great blessing, they do not substitute for our personal meditation in the words of Torah to derive personal inspiration and understanding (our own food).

6) The Eagle has amazing vision, being able to see another eagle or an enemy from 50 miles away. It has tremendous clarity and long distance focus. It sees the bigger picture, not just what is immediately in front of it. How important for a successful life.

7) The Eagle has a tremendous power to endure and renew itself. When an eagle reaches the age of 30, his physical condition begins to deteriorate. This aging process causes his talons to lose flexibility, his beak to become dull and his wing feathers to lose their luster and become heavy.

However, the eagle does not become 'depressed' by this condition and resign himself to an early death. By no means! He will instead fly to an isolated mountain top and over a five month period, go through a complete renewal. He will knock off his own beak by beating it on the rocks, pluck out his own talons and then his feathers. Each stage of 'pruning' if you will, produces a brand new version of the removed body part and at the end of 5 months, the eagle goes on to live (re-born) for another 30-40 years. Is it any wonder that the prophet Isaiah wrote, *"They that wait upon Hashem will renew their strength; their youth will be renewed like the eagles..."*

The Children of Israel, then and now, need to learn well the lessons of the Eagle in order that we may fulfill our mission as Hashem's chosen nation.

In Tune with Torah: To spend some time meditating on these various characteristics of the Eagle and to correct any attitudes we may have let creep into our thinking that are inconsistent with the principles we learn from this amazing creation.

Personal Thoughts

Mishpatim
Shemot/Exodus 21:1 – 24:18

The opening verse of this Torah portion alerts us that a transition is happening. To date, the Torah has been primarily narrative, informing and explaining to us the stories of the patriarchs, the slavery in Egypt, the Exodus, etc. This week, the Torah shifts to outlining the mitzvot which Hashem gives to Israel. In fact, in this parsha there are 53 commandments. Only one other parsha has more, Ki Tetzei in the last book of the Torah, Devarim, has 74.

Hashem tells Moshe, *'And these are the ordinances that you shall set before them..."* This short verse contains a very important message about the commandments. It is not enough to teach people what to do without explaining to them the deeper reasons and ideas contained within the Torah's instructions.

Human beings seek purpose, relevance and direction in life. A rote, uninspired presentation of Torah leaves a person 'cold'; simple lists of do's and don'ts with no inspiration or motivation turns people off and causes them to stray from the path of Torah to seek meaning elsewhere. Hashem's Torah is meant to be a spiritual feast, a banqueting table of food for a meaningful and fulfilling life.

Continuing to the next verse, we find something quite surprising. Given that the Children of Israel have just been delivered from slavery with miracles, we would expect the Torah to abolish slavery in no uncertain terms. However, in the very next verse we read the guidelines that must be observed if a Hebrew purchases another Hebrew to be his slave! What !?!?!? How are we to understand this??

There is no doubt that the value system of the Torah disapproves of arbitrary power of one human being over another human being. Even Hashem Himself did not -- and does not -- coerce people into embracing His Torah. We choose to do so. Why then does this perplexing verse appear at this juncture?

Our Creator knows well that people can change but that inner change takes time. A fundamental principle of our relationship with Him is that He does not force us to change faster than we choose to of our own free will. In context, Hashem is dealing with a nation of ex-slaves who have only been 'free' for three months after more than 200 years of enslavement. As the old saying goes, 'you can take the slave out of Egypt but it is something else to take Egypt out of the slave.'

Therefore, this commandment does not abolish slavery in one instant BUT it does set into motion a series of instructions designed to lead His people to do away with slavery of their own accord. Look at verses 2-6 in chapter 21 of Shemot/Exodus.

1) Slavery is to be no longer a permanent position but is now a temporary situation, lasting no more than 6 years. In the 7th year, the slave must go free.

2) Freedom comes not because of the benevolence of the master, but by Divine Command.

3) If the slave refuses to go free, the master is to pierce his ear at the doorpost, publicly. Why?

The ear that heard Hashem's voice at Sinai knows that slavery is not what Hashem wants for His people, that each Jew is a servant of Hashem, that to enslave oneself to another human being is to fall short of Hashem's will. Therefore, the 'slave by choice' will carry a physical reminder that he has chosen less than Hashem's will for his life. In effect, Hashem is saying to this 'slave by choice', "For whatever reason you are not ready to accept freedom, I give you six (or more) years to deal with your inner issues, confront your fears or insecurities, and prepare yourself for freedom because in the end, you **will** be free."

Ah, but you say, it says that the person who has his ear pierced will be a slave 'forever'. What do you mean, six or more years?

The Torah can never contradict itself. Later in the Torah, we read about the Year of Jubilee when everyone must return to his family, his home, etc. The 'slave by choice' remains in that state ONLY until the Jubilee Year. Then he MUST go free regardless. So if he chooses to remain a slave after the first 6 years, and there are yet another 39 years or 27 years or 19 years until the next Jubilee year, the Torah is saying that it is 'like' forever.

This commandment brings up an important issue that is as relevant today as it was then, and it is this:

Not every slave wants to go free.

We see it in the children of Israel who wanted to go back to the *"garlic, the leeks and the onions..."* of Egypt.

The truth is that internal slavery is the most insidious of all. We enslave ourselves to "what other people think about me", to appearance, to 'image', to negativity, to fear, to jealousy and envy, to all manner of thinking that paralyzes our ability to grow in maturity, holiness and righteousness. This week's parsha calls us to ask ourselves who or what enslaves us? And -- is there anyone that we 'enslave' with our prejudice, attitude or opinion?

The fear of freedom is a fear of accountability because Freedom, while giving us a sense of independence, also makes us feel insecure if we are unwilling to take full responsibility for ourselves, our decisions and our lifestyle. Some people find it just too stressful to think for themselves!

In the morning Blessings prayed by devout Jews each day, we bless Hashem "for not making me a slave" and later in the same series of Blessings, we bless Him for "releasing the imprisoned." Why are both of these blessings contained within the same prayer? Because though Hashem did not create us to be slaves, we enslave ourselves by our thinking and attitudes and therefore, we need to bless Him as the One who releases all who are imprisoned, beginning with ourselves.

In Tune with Torah: Summon up the courage to face any and every way of thinking within you that enslaves you in some degree or other. Resolve to take practical, doable steps towards the freedom Hashem desires for you.

Personal Thoughts

Terumah
Shemot/Exodus 25:1 – 27:19

In this portion of the Torah, Hashem begins to instruct Moshe on the building of the Tabernacle. We don't have to read far into the parsha to notice a marked emphasis on details - very specific details.

Some commentators have at times given the impression of being a bit bogged down with the specificity of each verse, wondering at its relevance today when compared with some of the more dramatic narratives of the Torah.

Traditionally, we are told, the details of the building of the Tabernacle mirror the details of Creation. Modern science has proven that the mathematical precision inherent in creation is absolutely essential to the ongoing functioning of this universe as we know it. Very precise details do in fact matter greatly to our Creator.

But let's go back for a moment to the giving of the Torah at Sinai. It was Hashem's original intent that Israel as a people would be a living Tabernacle of His presence in the earth; that as we fulfilled our declaration, *"We will do and we will hear"*, that the nations would see and know Almighty G-d through us.

Tragically, our ancestors fell all too soon from their exalted spiritual position at Sinai demonstrated by the event of the Golden Calf. It became glaringly apparent that the children of Israel needed a visible, tangible example before their eyes of the essence of their calling as a nation. That visible, tangible example was the Tabernacle.

Hashem instructed Moshe to *"build a Sanctuary for Me..."*, a place where His glory could be manifest and expressed, a place that would stand at the very center of the Tribes of Israel day and night, that would travel with them and would continually remind them that just as the Tabernacle was brilliant with His presence in a barren place, so, too, Israel's calling is to be a bright and enduring spiritual Light to the Nations in every generation.

Building a life that reflects Hashem's goodness and love requires every bit as much attention to detail as building a home...or building the Tabernacle.

There is a vast difference between building a house and building a home. While it is a given that construction of a house is a process including myriads of small and large details, building a home is an even greater challenge. I have seen, as have you, some beautiful homes designed and built by fine construction companies which nevertheless stand empty, for no one lives there.

Building a home requires not just the physical structure but very specific qualities in the values, attitudes and behaviors of the human beings that live within that structure. And herein is the secret of the Tabernacle.

Each detail outlined in this week's parsha contains within it a dimension of holy living designed to speak to every generation of Jews about how we -- individually and corporately -- become a living Tabernacle of the presence of Hashem in this world. Let's take just one example - the Menorah.

Formed from one solid piece of gold, it was fashioned very specifically to give maximum light. It is beyond the scope of a brief commentary like this one to elaborate on every detail but suffice it to say that the type of 'LIGHT' that we are called to share with the rest of the world is seven-fold, just as the Menorah had seven branches: the light of truth, the light of peace, the light of joy in serving Hashem, the light of wisdom, the light of Torah, the light of Hashem's love. When you and I walk through life according to Hashem's truth, in tune with His Torah, implementing the wisdom we have learned from the

Torah into our decisions and actions, at peace with Hashem and with those around us, allowing the joy of serving Him to spread to others, we become progressively a brighter and brigher living Menorah, giving light to the world.

This is but a small and simple example of the deep truths contained in this parsha and I encourage you, I urge you to seek out through prayer, meditation and study the awesome life lessons embedded in the verses of Terumah.

In tune with Torah: This is a good day to renew your personal commitment to be a living Tabernacle of His presence and to seek new ways to express that reality through your daily life.

Personal Thoughts

Tetzaveh
Shemot/Exodus 27:20 – 30:10

This week's Torah portion, Tetzaveh, brings to the forefront something very special about Hashem's relationship with His people.

Throughout the centuries, discussion has abounded as to why Hashem created the world in the first place. A key phrase to answer that question was found in last week's parsha, "They will make for Me a sanctuary and I will dwell in their midst." The Midrash, commenting on this verse, says "G-d had a passion to have for Himself a dwelling place in the lower world." (Naso 16)

With this in mind, Rabbi Avraham Aryeh Trugman writes in his book, Orchard of Delights, that we can look at the Tabernacle as a fulfillment of Hashem's 'passion' to have a dwelling place on this earth among His chosen people. In commanding the building of the Tabernacle, Hashem provided Himself with a place, a location, where He could be approached and tangibly experienced by the people, and on the other hand, a place where in a mysterious way, He could approach and experience His creation.

That, in essence, was the purpose for the Tabernacle and for the Temples. They were designed to be meeting places between G-d and man. The physical structures and the services performed within them were ultimately meant to be a visible reminder, a symbol of the sanctuary He desired to be built within each human being, body and soul, mind and heart. When this is accomplished, the entire purpose of creation will be fulfilled. Then will the "knowledge of Hashem cover the earth like the waters cover the sea..."

World religions and philosophies in general tend to lean in one of two ways. Some place enormous emphasis on the earthly and the here and now; others seek to obscure the present creation with great emphasis on the hereafter, the world to come. In simple terms, some are so earthly-minded, they are no heavenly good and others are so heavenly minded, they are no earthly good.

The Tabernacle is meant, among other things, to teach us to strive for balance in our life, to combine heaven and earth into a beautiful harmony. It is our job to embrace, appreciate and enjoy Hashem's creation on this earth with gratitude and to sanctify this creation that it may bring honor to Him. It is just as much our job to anticipate with joy the inestimable pleasures of His presence in the World to

Come. It is written in Pirkei Avot (Ethics of the Fathers) that "This world is like a lobby before the World to Come. Prepare yourself in the lobby so that you may enter the banquet hall." 4:16

Each day is a gift to be used for uniting heaven and earth in whatever way we can during that day. Hashem's presence in the world is enhanced as we do so.

In Tune with Torah: elevating even the most mundane thing we do by doing it with joy as our service to Hashem, that His creation reflect His goodness a little bit more today because of how I go about my daily life. This is how you and I participate in seeing His passion realized - a dwelling place for Him in the lower world. May it be so for all of us.

Personal Thoughts

Ki Tissa
Shemot/Exodus 30:11 – 34:35

Hashem said to Moshe, 'Speak to the Israelites and say to them: you must keep my Sabbaths. It is a sign between Me and you for all generations to make you realize that I, Hashem, am making you holy.' Shemot/Exodus 31:12-13

After outlining the instructions for the Mishkan (Tabernacle), Hashem repeated the commandment to keep Shabbat for the second time to insure that the children of Israel would not think that Shabbat could be ignored while they were building the Mishkan. After all, the Mishkan was being built to house the Divine Presence in the midst of the people. One could think that perhaps that was more important than Shabbat, at least temporarily during the building process. Therefore, Hashem impressed upon Moshe to tell the people that Shabbat must still be kept.

We cannot overemphasize the pre-eminence of Shabbat. The very first Shabbat was observed by Hashem Himself as we read in Beresheit, *"And Hashem rested on the seventh day."* 2:2 Since Hashem created the entire world with speech, it certainly was not a matter of resting from arduous physical labor! Aha! Perhaps herein is an aspect of Shabbat that is too little discussed!

When the Torah says, "Hashem rested from His work..." it is telling us that throughout the seventh day, Hashem uttered NO creative words as He had been doing for the previous six days. Nothing new came into being on the seventh day. There was quiet, stillness, peace, tranquility. This is the fundamental meaning of the Hebrew word, menuha, usually translated as 'rest'.

Have we realized that an integral part of observing Shabbat involves the faculty of speech? The world was created because "God said....and it was so. That was His 'work'.

The immediately obvious application is that we should refrain from any creative expression like writing a poem, for example, which would 'create' something that has not existed before; or discussing business ventures or financial planning and other such topics that occupy our attention during the other six days of the week. But is there anything else?

We know that we are not to kindle a fire in our homes on Shabbat so devout Jews refrain from such activities as cooking, taking care to prepare Shabbat food ahead of time. But what about the 'fire' that can be kindled by the human tongue? If we are scrupulously careful to avoid literally 'kindling a fire' in our homes, but are careless with the manner in which we speak to our spouses, children or other family members on the Sabbath, are we truly observing the commandment? Are the efforts made by devout Jews to guard against kindling a fire in their homes purely an external, mechanical issue? I would suggest, rather, that refraining from actually kindling fire (such as with one's oven or fireplace) should serve as a weekly reminder to keep our speech gentle, calm and loving, most especially throughout Shabbat.

Should we not do so every day? Certainly, but who among us would dare claim to have reached such a lofty level of spirituality? It would be a worthy undertaking to focus on keeping Shabbat as Hashem did, by resting from idle chatting and devoting ourselves to uplifting conversation, such as discussion of Torah.

We derive from the text a second reason that Hashem repeated the commandment to keep Shabbat. "It is a sign between Me and you for all generations to make you realize that I, Hashem, am making you holy."

Should the people have been allowed to think that the work of the Tabernacle superceded Shabbat, they could have concluded that Hashem's holiness rested in a structure made of wood, stone and fabric. It was paramount that they know the truth; i.e., that holiness was to be in them. "You shall make Me a Sanctuary and I shall dwell in them." Israel was to be the living Tabernacle of which the Mishkan was to be a visible example and reminder.

The word 'holy' (Kadosh in Hebrew) first appears in Bresheit when Hashem set apart the seventh day and called it 'holy'. Living as we do in a world of material things which occupy so much of our attention on a daily basis, it is most significant to note that the first thing God called 'holy' was not a thing, but a period of time. Observing Shabbat, in the words of Abraham Joshua Heschel, is the art of creating a palace in time, a palace when our soul reconnects in a dynamic way with its Creator, the King of the Universe.

It was imperative that the children of Israel know that it was not the Tabernacle that would make them holy; Hashem was making them holy and the first 'location' of holiness He created was not a geographical place such as the Tabernacle, but a location in time, Shabbat.

As noted in last week's commentary, Hashem knew that the Tabernacle would not last forever; neither would the Temples in Jerusalem. But nothing can do away with Shabbat. That is why it -- and it alone -- is a 'sign between Me and you for all generations...'

If there is no Mishkan, every week there is still Shabbat. If there is no Temple, every week there is still Shabbat. It is taught that whoever keeps Shabbat is considered as if he kept the entire Torah.

However long we study, there is always more to learn about the great gift of Shabbat.

In tune with Torah: observing Shabbat consistently with all our heart and soul, drawing to ourselves the special holiness of the seventh day, to refocus our minds and hearts on what is truly important.

May "Shabbat Shalom" become much more than a greeting, may it be for each of us a deeply spiritual experience.

Personal Thoughts

Vayakhel
Shemot/Exodus 35:1 – 38:20

Didn't we just read the Torah's account of the construction of the Tabernacle in the past couple of weeks? Yet, here it is again in this week's Torah portion. Even our great commentator, Rashi, refers us to his previous expositions on the building of the Tabernacle (see Rashi 35:5) and writes very little with reference to Vayakhel.

Yet, we are aware that the Torah does not waste space with even one extra letter, let alone entire sections. Why then, the repetition?

Could it be that the name of this week's Torah portion, "Vayakhel", gives us a clue to answer this question?

In general, we do ascribe significance to the names of the Torah portions. It is not simply a pragmatic device to create a name from one of the first few words of the portion. Even if the custom did develop in such a fashion, the very fact that the Jewish People collectively accepted these names for the weekly Torah portions does have significance.

What then does the name "Vayakhel" signify? "(And he (Moshe) congregated")

Let's take a look at a passage of Talmud:

From where do we draw the understanding that the Divine Presence is with a group of ten (a minyan) praying? Because the verse in Psalms 82, says, "God stands with His assembly."

From where do we conclude that God is with two people when they study Torah together? Because the verse in Malachi 3 states, "Then the God-fearing men spoke, each one to his friend, and God listened."

And from where do we know that even when one person studies Torah, God is with him? Because the verse in Exodus 20, says, "In every place that My Name is mentioned, I will come to you and bless you."

Now since we know that God's Presence is with even one person, why do we need to look for other verses to conclude that God is with two or ten people? The answer is that God writes a group of two in His Book of Remembrances, while an individual's study is not written there. With a group of ten, God actually comes to them before they start praying. (Babylonian Talmud, Brachot 6a)

Is there something about this quote from the Talmud that raises an eyebrow? How can we suggest that God only writes down the Torah study of a group of two? Don't we pray on Rosh Hashana for God to inscribe us in His Book of Life, whether or not we are with a group? Besides, we read in Pirkei Avot (Ethics of the Fathers) that "All of our actions are recorded in His book."

The answer is that the Talmud passage quoted above agrees that all of our actions are written down in God's book. But when we study with a partner, the action is recorded in its own separate book.

The explanation is that when a group does a Mitzvah together, it is quite a different spiritual reality than if an individual performs a holy deed by himself. We are well acquainted with the concept of the power of unity in prayer, for example. It is not a matter simply of quantity. Rather, that action is qualitatively different in the eyes of God when it is undertaken by a group of people unanimously committed to the same outcome. Therefore, it warrants being recorded in a separate heavenly book.

We have all probably heard before that the word "team" stands for 'Together Everyone Accomplishes More'. Teamwork or working as a community yields a level of success in ways that are beyond the ability of individuals to produce. Team sports as well as group projects prove this principle consistently.

It is the same in the spiritual realm. The quality of the Mitzvah will be far richer when performed by a group and God credits the Mitzvah as such in Heaven. Therefore we also read in Pirkei Avot (4:14), "A group gathering for the sake of heaven is so powerful that it is guaranteed to have lasting effects."

So why does Torah repeat the details of the construction of the Tabernacle? To reinforce the reality of the power of community.

Shemot, the Book of Exodus, is all about the creation of the Jewish People as a Community. It is in Exodus where we come together as a Nation, found in slavery, and delivered into freedom for a Divine Purpose.

It is in Shemot that we accept the Torah at Sinai and receive our national mission to be a "light to the world." Is it not appropriate then to approach the close of the book of Exodus with the glowing national achievement of bringing God's Presence into the world through the Tabernacle?

Though the details of constructing the Tabernacle were covered in earlier Torah portions, now that it is completed, God wants to stress to His people that no one individual could have created this sanctuary, but as a unified community, as a nation in whom everyone contributed their portion, we have built the Mishkan.

Israel is more than the sum of its individual members. The nation as a whole is a divine creation of God Himself for a purpose that affects the entire world.

This is why the Parsha is called Vayakhel. *"And he (Moshe) congregated."* The key to the entire portion is to understand the importance of a congregation and its spiritually powerful actions. The Jewish People fulfilled their mission in bringing God into the world through the Tabernacle and they did it as a community, not as millions of individuals. So God writes every detail of the construction of the Tabernacle "again" because He wants us to appreciate it as well.

In Tune with Torah = may our reading of Parshat VaYakhel impress anew upon our souls the beautiful power of community and teamwork in all aspects of our lives.

Personal Thoughts

Pekudei

Shemot/Exodus 38:21 – 40:38

As the Mishkan is now completed, Moshe sees that all God's instructions have been carried out precisely, and he blesses the people: *"And Moshe looked upon all the work, and, behold, they had done it as God had commanded, so had they done it; and Moshe blessed them.* (Shemot 39:43)

The purpose of the Tabernacle was to create a house of prayer, a 'residence' for the Shechina. It seems more than appropriate that Moshe would bless the people for this accomplishment.

But, have you ever wondered what Moshe actually said in his blessing? Our Sage, Rashi, suggests that this prayer was preserved in our liturgy, and is familiar to us even today: *"And Moshe blessed them: he said to them, "May it be [God's] will that the Shechina rest on the work of your hands, and may the pleasantness of the Almighty our God be upon us..."* (Tehilim/Psalm 90) This is one of the eleven Psalms attributed to Moshe in the Book of Psalms.

This particular psalm is an eloquent prayer that could be uttered by anyone on completing any project. When we work hard and succeed in creating something worthwhile, the spiritual response of a humble, honest person is a prayer that God bless the work of his hands. However, there is much more in this Psalm than a general prayer for success.

God, you have been our dwelling place in all generations... May the pleasantness of the Almighty our God be upon us; and establish the work of our hands upon us; O prosper it, the work of our hands. (Psalm 90)

Look how this Psalm speaks directly of the purpose of the just-completed Mishkan as a physical expression of God's Presence among the People of Israel. No wonder Rashi associated this Psalm with the prayer Moshe spoke upon seeing the completed Mishkan, the manifestation of the peoples' precise and careful attention to God's instructions.

It is difficult for our earthly minds to properly evaluate human achievements. For example, think for a moment of the Tabernacle, the First Temple and the Second Temple. Human reasoning would be inclined to think that the Second Temple was the greatest of the three structures for it contained the most gold by weight of all three. The First Temple would come in second on the basis of this measurement and the Tabernacle would be third.

However, the Torah reality is that the Mishkan was more holy than the first Beit Hamikdash, which was, in turn, holier than the Second Temple. The quantity of gold had nothing to do with its spiritual value!

God measures value by the condition of the hearts of the people who stood behind the actual process of erecting each structure. The Mishkan was built by a man named Bezalel, a man whose entire being was permeated with the spirit of God; hence the edifice which he erected was infused with the spirit of God. The first Temple was built by foreign workers commissioned for the project. The Second Temple was built by Herod.

The Tabernacle was build by inspired men who focused exclusively on Hashem's will to its minutest detail. The holiness of their obedience permeated the finished structure.

Therefore, just as God blessed the world when Creation was complete, so Moshe blessed the Mishkan when it was complete.

As the book of Shemot comes to a close, as the Mishkan stands, ready to serve as a dwelling for God among us and as a place where every Jew can reconnect with the spirituality and love experienced at Sinai, Moshe blesses those who took part in the project, and, indirectly, all of us.

In Tune with Torah = May all of our thoughts, words, motivations and actions be imbued with holiness. May He who dwelt in the Mishkan, the Same One who has been our refuge throughout all generations, nourish the reality of community, love, peace and friendship among us; lead us into our final redemption and the rebuilding of God's earthly Tabernacle, even in our days and say, Amen.

Personal Thoughts

Vayikra/Leviticus

The Third Book
Of the Torah

Vayikra
Vayikra/Leviticus 1:1 – 5:26

We now begin the third book of the Torah - Vayikra/Leviticus. The reader immediately notices that this book is completely different from the previous ones as its focus is on the Temple sacrifices and offerings while the previous two books contained primarily narrative.

Mention of "sacrifices" oftentimes raises questions; modern man finds it a difficult concept. One of the questions sometimes asked is this: How is it that prayer is now considered a "substitute" for the Temple sacrifices? Isn't that an "addition" to Torah which the Torah itself prohibits?

A careful study of Vayikra teaches us that atonement for sin consists of both animal sacrifices AND sincere confession accompanied by repentant prayer in conjunction with the sacrifice. From the beginning, the Torah commanded sincere repentance as a means of atonement. To simply bring a sacrifice to the Temple without a change of heart provided NO benefit. In biblical times, atonement prayer was fully sanctioned by God, with or without animal offerings for Jews and non-Jews alike as can be seen in Jonah 3:5-10.

Therefore, let's settle the question.

No, the Rabbis did not "add to the Torah" when they emphasized repentant prayer as a means of obtaining forgiveness and atonement. It is a Torah principle that the primary means for obtaining atonement when animal sacrifices cannot be offered concurrently is repentant prayer.

As a matter of fact, Scripture declares clearly that animal sacrifices are only prescribed for accidental or unintentional sin (see Leviticus 4:2, 13, 22, 27; 5:5, 15 (cf. Numbers 15:30). Deliberate, intentional sin can only be atoned for through repentance, unaccompanied by a blood sacrifice- Psalms 32:5, 51:16-19.

Following the destruction of the Second Temple in 70 C.E., it was no longer possible to continue the sacrificial system, but no innovation was necessary, only a readjustment of what already existed.

We see the efficacy of repentance with prayer proven in history. During the Babylonian exile, after the Israelites repented they were allowed to return to their homeland. Yet, they had no means of offering a blood sacrifice; they could only offer contrite repentant prayer.

146

According to the book of 1 Maccabees (cf. 1:54, 4:52) valid sacrifices in the Temple were discontinued for three years (168-165 B.C.E.). This meant those loyal to God could not offer personal atonement sacrifices in the Temple. During these periods of time, no Temple sacrifice was possible. Did God leave these Jews in their sins, with no means whatsoever for atonement? Not at all! The same God who gave the Torah spoke to the exiles in Babylonia through the prophet Jeremiah: "And you shall call upon Me, and go, and pray to Me, and I will hearken to you. And you shall seek Me, and find Me, when you shall search for Me with all your heart" (Jeremiah 29:13).

Thus, the Temple's destruction caused a modification, not an innovation, for the Torah provided ahead of time the answer to the question, "How will the Jews receive atonement if the Temple is destroyed?"

The inability to offer animal sacrifices causes no interruption in the divine flow of forgiveness and atonement for sin. Biblically, confession and repentant prayer can and does satisfy all the criteria necessary for attaining God's forgiveness even without the presence of a blood sacrifice.

So what do we learn from this? That God has NEVER left His people without the means for receiving forgiveness of sin. As God had always permitted, and continues to do to our very day, anyone may come to Him with sincere repentance in contrite prayer.

The rabbis were absolutely correct to implement the biblically prescribed method to be followed when no blood sacrifice offering is possible. Repentant prayer, the offering of the lips, is not a man-made alternative to offering a blood sacrifice; it is an essential Torah mandated foundation of God's relationship with Israel, whom He will never abandon or cast away.

In Tune with Torah: may God grant to all of us a deeper appreciation of the power of prayer, especially repentant prayer, and the discipline to devote ourselves to it with renewed fervor.

Personal Thoughts

Tzav
Vayikra/Leviticus 6:1- 8:36

This week's parsha opens with the description of a rather odd commandment. The cohen(priest) is commanded to remove the ashes from the previous day's sacrifices that have burned on the altar all night, and carry them out of the Mishkan (Tabernacle) to a designated place outside the camp.

Essentially, the priest is being told to take out the garbage. Of course, this is not ordinary garbage – these are the remnants of the sacrifices offered to Hashem.

Now, we may have expected this work to be done by a custodian, or the equivalent of a minimum wage worker. Yet we are told that this act was performed by the kohanim, the priests – the most privileged people in the Temple.

Rabbi Samson Raphael Hirsch, the leading figure of the 19th Century German Orthodox community wrote that we should not think the removal of ashes from the altar is simply a preparatory stage for the new day's Temple service. Rather, it is the final conclusion of the previous day's service.

We all understand that the need for continuity from one day to the next is crucial. However, there is a danger in placing too much emphasis on yesterday – the danger of living in the past, either positively by congratulating ourselves on what we have already accomplished -- or negatively, by dwelling on past failures or mistakes. This, explains Rav Hirsch, is why there was a need for the ritual of removing the ashes from the Temple. He explains: "The thought of what has already been accomplished can be the death of that which is still to be accomplished. Woe unto him who, with smug self-complacency thinks he can rest on his laurels, on what he has already achieved, and who does not meet the task of every fresh day with full fresh devotion as if it were the first day of his life's work!"

We must live with a delicate balance. On the one hand, our current responsibilities are in fact connected with and a continuation of the previous work; on the other hand, we cannot place too strong of an emphasis on the past and what we have already accomplished but we must greet each new day with fresh energy, vision and focus for each day is a world of its own. Each new day presents us with fresh opportunity to serve God with all our heart, soul and strength.

Time is a precious gift; the present is what we have in which to honor God and to grow in holiness. Yesterday is gone; tomorrow is not yet ours. Today is the gift in our hands, the opportunity to take what the past has taught us and be better, kinder, holier this day than we were yesterday.

This is the same balance we seek to achieve at the Pesach seder. On the one hand, we come to the seder with a very strong sense of history. We tell the story of what happened to our ancestors thousands of years ago in Egypt. Yet, our goal is not merely to tell the story and focus on the past.

As we read in the Haggadah, "In every generation a person must see him/herself as if he/she personally went out of Egypt." We must make the story and message of Pesach relevant to us in our current situation.

Furthermore, we express our desire to say before Hashem a "new song" (shirah chadashah) because the praise that we say to God once we have made the story of Pesach relevant and applicable to our lives is a brand new, unprecedented song of praise for God.

It is also why we celebrate Purim. The deliverance of the Jewish people achieved by the heroism of Queen Esther is not just history. It is also a personal challenge to each of us to play our part in the ongoing deliverance of Israel from her enemies. Perhaps you and I are not in a position of authority as Esther was. But each of us has the ability and responsibility to pray as Esther requested of Mordecai and all the people in face of the existential threat posed in her day.

Today is no different. The God of Israel has kept His covenant with Israel throughout all her generations -- and He will do so forever, for that is His promise. But He also asks and expects that we seek Him with all our heart and soul. This is our part, our work of service.

In Tune with Torah: gratitude for all that Hashem has done for us in the past coupled with dedication to live each day to its fullest, serving Him with the kind of devotion and enthusiasm that makes each day count. May we all be delivered from the tragedy of a half-lived life.

Personal Thoughts

Shemini
Vayikra/Leviticus 9:1 – 11:47

This Torah portion is found in Vayikra/Leviticus chapters 9 through 11. It begins with the words, *'It was on the eighth day...'*

The number 8 in Gematria (biblical numerology) carries the meaning of 'new beginnings', 'a new order of things', and 'the first of a new series'. We see this played out in the very first chapter of the Torah which describes the creation of the world in 6 days followed by the day of rest -- Shabbat -- on the 7th day. The next day or the 8th day is in fact the first day of the system of weeks which was a 'new order of things'.

Jewish baby boys are circumcised on the 8th day after their birth, thereby entering into the covenant.

We also note that after the Flood in the days of Noah, 8 souls survived to begin the 'new order of things' - to repopulate the earth and create a new society after the devastation.

The events described in Vayikra/Lev. 10:1 - 3 happen on this same 8th day which is referenced in the opening verse of this portion. This particular 8th day also held great significance. It immediately followed the time of instructions regarding the various types of sacrifices which we read in last week's parsha. Having been taught what to do, the time has now come to do it on this 8th day.

What was so unique about this day?

1 - It was the first day for the priesthoos to serve in the Mishkan/Tabernacle

2 - It was the first day for the Divine Service in which communal offerings would be presented to Hashem

3 - It was the first day that the leaders of each Tribe would bring sacrifices (ref. Num. 7:10)

4 - It was the first day that heavenly fire descended and consumed the sacrifices.

5 - It was the first day that the Divine Presence rested on the Mishkan in the midst of Israel

6 - It was the first day that the Israelites would be blessed with the Priestly Blessing by Aaron.

7 - It was the first day on which private altars for sacrifice were prohibited

8 - It was Rosh Chodesh Nissan - the first day of the month Nissan which is the first month of the biblical year.

Another series of '8'.

Against this unique background, two of the sons of Aaron the Kohen Gadol (High Priest), Nadav and Abihu, bring their fire pans with what the Torah calls "foreign fire" and present it to God, a fire which God had not commanded to be brought on this hallmark day. For this transgression, they suffer immediate death.

Wow - one may react. What a harsh punishment! How can this be? Were not these young men virtuous, dedicated, passionate about God and His Torah? In fact, yes, they were. So what went wrong?

First of all, they offered foreign fire on a particularly sacred day, making their transgression all the more serious.

Secondly, theirs was a great calling. With great gifting comes great responsibility and accountability.

Thirdly, wise men have taught us that our greatest strengths can become our downfall.

Zeal for God and the Torah is a very good thing; excessive zeal leads to spiritual pride, haughtiness and a sense of superiority. Excessive zeal leads one to go beyond what God has commanded and the Torah tells us "not to add or subtract" from His Word. A misguided passion can distort the ultra-religious mindset into thinking that "doing more" is better, holier, and superior to others, thereby feeding the human tendency towards self-exaltion. Pride results from a bloated sense of self-importance.

One of Judaism's greatest sages, Rabbi Moshe Chaim Luzzato, wrote in his classic work, THE PATH OF THE JUST (MESSILAT YESHARIM):

Our Sages of blessed memory have said (Sotah 5b), "How great are those who are lowly in spirit, for when the Beit HaMikdash [Temple] was in existence a person would sacrifice a burnt offering and would be credited for the burnt offering, [or] a meal offering and be credited for a meal offering. Yet he who is humble of mind is considered as if he has sacrificed all of the offerings possible, as it says in Tehillim 51:19, 'the [preferred] Divine sacrifices are those of a broken spirit.' This is the praise given to the humble in spirit, for they possess humilty in their hearts and thoughts."

Far be it from us to arbitrarily judge the heart intent of Nadav and Abihu in bringing their "foreign fire", but we must seek to learn from their experience. One lesson among others is our need to walk humbly before God and our fellow man; to guard our hearts against any attitude of superiority, intolerance, or disrespect towards those whose spiritual path may differ from ours; to flee from "holier than thou" thoughts, words or deeds that feed pride and destroy humility.

In Tune with Torah: nurturing an attitude of respect towards others while realizing that regardless of how far we may have come in our own spirituality, we still have a great deal of growing to do.

Personal Thoughts

Tazria
Vayikra/Leviticus 12:1 – 13:58

Most of this Torah Portion entitled Tazria outlines the principles and conditions regarding tzoraas, when white blotches appear on a person's skin. He or she must then undergo a set time of isolation from others followed by a process of purification.

This affliction on the skin is actually the third stage of afflictions which this parsha teaches. We also learn that one's home might be 'afflicted' and one's clothing as well, before the affliction actually touches the person themselves. This three fold progression is actually a manifestation of Hashem's mercy in judgment. He gives two opportunities to get our attention, so to speak, before touching our bodies themselves for the purpose of bringing us to repentance.

The Talmud delineates seven sins whose severity could bring this type of judgment: slander, murder, perjury, jealousy, theft, immorality and pride. One is quick to notice that 'lashon hora' (negative or evil speech) is associated overtly or covertly with all seven of these sins. Therefore we are taught that such afflictions often stem from this very sin. The 'judgment' or affliction that ensues is designed by Hashem to demonstrate the destructiveness of one's sin and persuade the person to repent and resolve to avoid sinning in such a way again.

It seems that there are two lessons in particular that one who speaks 'lashon hara' is taught during the period of his 'suffering'.

Firstly, the Talmud tells us, "he caused separation between man and his friend [through his evil speech and therefore the Torah said that he must sit alone." Speaking negatively about others inevitably causes rifts between people and disrupts friendships, and sometimes even marriages. Therefore, measure for measure, one who speaks 'lashon hara' is forced to live alone for a period of time, separated from others, to learn by experience the pain that is caused by damaging relationships.

Secondly, the physical manifestations (whether severe mold growing on one's walls, or rashes and blotches on one's skin, for example) are meant to show visibly the kind of damage done to one's soul by speaking lashon hora. Tzoraas, as described in the Torah, is not actually a regular physical illness, but an outward display of an inner spiritual problem.

Nowadays there is no 'tzoraas' in the classic sense described in this week's parsha. However, should we not consider that perhaps we are missing important messages from Hashem when we do not look beyond the surface of things that happen in our lives and treat them simply as a physical nuisance. Tzoraas was a form of loving kindness from God in that He communicated very clearly to the sinner regarding his transgression and the need to repent.

The Talmud acknowledges that some people stumble in immorality, others in jealousy and others in theft, but everyone commits lashon hora. Without tzoraas today, how can a person recognize the spiritual damage one causes himself when he speaks 'lashon hara' and the extent of the damage that negative words can have on other people?

Judaism teaches that there is a reason for everything that happens. Often, the reason may not be immediately apparent but if we will ask God for insight, He will give it to us. Therefore, the humble heart will always be ready to inquire of God: "What are you saying to me?" when confronted with any form of 'affliction' - whether in one's home, one's possessions or one's person.

With regard to 'lashon hora', there is another source of help. Because of the unique importance of avoiding this particular sin, we highly recommend a wonderful book, **A Lesson A Day**, a daily devotional on the topic of proper and godly speech. It is a compilation of the teachings of Rabbi Yisrael Meir Kagan, also known as the Chofetz Chaim. It is a magnificent addition to anyone's spiritual library and provides immeasurable help, insight and inspiration for improving one's speech in daily life.

In Tune with Torah: May we all be blessed with the ability to avoid all forms of negative speech. What particular challenges do you have in this regard? What steps can you take to improve?

Personal Thoughts

Metzora
Vayikra/Leviticus 14:1 – 15:33

Admittedly, this Torah portion is one that we might find difficult, containing as it does, commandments regarding the purification of someone afflicted with tzaraas (commonly translated as leprosy) which is virtually non-existent in the modern world. A surface reading leads some to suggest that there is little relevancy to the modern world in this portion. Not so, as we will see.

We learned last week that this condition -- tzaraas -- is not simply a physical illness but one that is associated with a spiritual cause, most notably it appears as a result of continued 'lashon hora' (evil speech). The person with this condition is called a "metzora."

The metzora was isolated outside the camp, away from the community, for a period of seven days, affording them an opportunity to ponder the seriousness of their sins and to repent. Stop and think a minute -- imagine how you might feel if you were cast out of the city where you live because of a moral failure, and made to sit alone for 7 days and 7 nights, totally isolated from human contact with anyone in your family or circle of friends. Imagine the thoughts, the remorse, and the fears you might have of how the community would look at you after the 7 days were completed. This was not an easy experience -- it wasn't meant to be.

At the conclusion of the period of isolation, the priest would take the penitent through the rituals of purification. It is notable that the priest, bound by numerous commandments prohibiting contact with any form of impurity, in this case goes out to the isolated individual. (See Lev. 14: 10-20)

Not only does he approach the metzora but he himself is the one who anoints the alienated one on the ear, the thumb and the right toe. He physically touches the metzora a) to say that the metzora retains no impurity and b) to restore the person's dignity and eliminate any residual stigma or shame.

Two weeks ago we read about the consecration of Aaron and his sons (Lev. 8: 23-24). In that ceremony, Moshe anointed the ear, the thumb and the right toe of those being dedicated to the high calling of serving as Priests in the Temple of the Holy One of Israel -- the very same ritual as that used for the purification of a repentant sinner! The same rituals that were used to confer Divine authority on priests -- and kings as well for that matter -- are used to restore the metzora to the community of Israel.

What a powerful picture of Hashem's lovingkindness and mercy!

The 'outcast' is not begrudgingly allowed back into the fold, but rather he is honored through the same rituals that dignify priests and kings. This ceremony conveys in bold display how Hashem looks upon those who repent. They are uplifted and honored before the community and restored to a place of full membership and status with the rest of Am Yisrael. He makes good on His promise to throw the sins of the repentant into the sea of His forgetfulness and to remember them no more. How great is the love of Hashem towards those who repent.

In the Torah, we are called a "nation of priests". In the context of Metzora, this should mean to us that we have the honor and the privilege of embracing with open arms those who repent and turn to Hashem after a "fall". There can be no place in our own attitudes for superiority, arrogance or self-righteousness, but rather a humility that rejoices at the mercy of Hashem on another's life and is truly happy when someone is reconciled to God. This is the way of the Jew.

But how do we "know" if they have truly repented? Perhaps we don't. However, it is incumbent upon us to give them the benefit of the doubt - and accept their confession of repentance, choosing to think the best of them, as we would want someone to do towards us. Maimonides taught that one only knows if he has truly repented when he is presented with the same opportunity to sin as before and successfully overcomes the temptation. That is for the person themselves to know - as for the rest of us, our response is to love, encourage and support.

In Tune with Torah: purging our minds of negative attitudes towards others; believing the best about them and walking in humility, knowing that there are none who have not sinned.

Personal Thoughts

Acharei Mot
Vayikra/Leviticus 16:1 – 18:30

This Portion is often read on the Shabbat which immediately precedes the beginning of Pesach/Passover, called "Shabbat HaGadol" - the Great Shabbat. How is it that this - of all the Sabbaths throughout the year - is the one chosen to be called "Great"?

In the 12th chapter of Shemot/Exodus we read that just prior to the Exodus Moshe instructed the children of Israel to choose a lamb for each household on the 10th of Nissan. The lamb was to be inspected during the subsequent days until the 14th of Nissan when it was to be slaughtered and eaten in the evening after sundown which according to the Hebrew calendar was the 15th of Nissan for the Hebrew day begins at sundown.

We know historically that the children of Israel left Egypt on a Thursday so the lambs were slaughtered on Wednesday, the 14th. Therefore they were chosen on the previous Saturday -- Shabbat -- the 10th of Nissan.

Shabbat existed from creation -- "and God rested on the seventh day..." but Shabbat was not mandated to the children of Israel until the Torah was given at Sinai. Therefore, while Israel was enslaved in Egypt, they had not yet been commanded to keep Shabbat.

THIS Shabbat, however, was the turning point. On the 10th of Nissan, in the year of the Exodus, for the very first time, Israel as a nation joined God in keeping Shabbat.

The Sages explain: the lamb was a sacred animal to the Egyptians; it was one of their many 'gods', comparable to the sacred cows today in India. For the enslaved Hebrews to take lambs from the Egyptians and slaughter them was the acid test of their faith in ONE God and in His servant, Moshe. By implementing this decree, the children of Israel rejected the idolatry with which they had been surrounded for more than 200 years and demonstrated their faith in Hashem by obeying a difficult and dangerous commandment.

This act of obedience is a pivotal point in Israel's history. It was the preparatory step towards Sinai, towards the majestic deliverance they were about to experience -- a deliverance which was not an end in itself, but the means through which they would be led to the place where they would experience history's greatest event - the giving of the Torah by

God Himself to the congregation of Israel at Mt. Sinai.

This was indeed the GREAT Shabbat!

It is also noteworthy that the Egyptians made no protest to the Hebrew slaves taking the lambs. They knew what was going to happen but after the previous nine plagues which they had experienced, the Egyptian people were afraid of the Hebrews. The "enslavers" had themselves become enslaved by fear of the God of the Hebrews.

In *Acharei Mot* we find this instruction: *"And you shall guard My observances..."* 18:30. It is from this verse and another similar one that the Sages derived the principle of developing what are called "fences" for the Torah -- rabbinical decrees whose purposes are to protect us from transgressing the Torah, particularly in areas of personal vulnerability.

The concept is well known to us. We put fences around swimming pools lest, G-d forbid, a child should fall in and accidentally drown. Fences are erected along narrow mountain roads lest, G-d forbid, an automobile should accidentally get to close to the edge and plunge over a cliff. The Torah instructs us elsewhere that if we build a house with a flat roof, we must put a fence around the roof lest someone accidentally fall off.

"Fences" around the Torah are designed to emphasize to us the seriousness of transgressing Hashem's instructions. They serve to help us, to protect us from our own weaknesses. Not every 'fence' is equally meaningful to every Jew for we are all different, with different strengths and weaknesses. What we need to understand is that every fence is significant and important to someone. Individually we are to be humbly thankful for those fences which help us individually to keep Hashem's Torah.

Take for example the well known practice of the lighting of two candles on Friday evening by the woman of the home to welcome Shabbat. You will not find that practice specifically mandated in the written Torah. However, it is a decree that serves a uniquely important function. Lighting two Shabbat candles on Friday evening expresses our commitment to obey the explicit command of the Torah to "observe" and "safeguard" the seventh day as a day set apart for Hashem. That moment is the cut off point between the six days of the week and the special day of Shabbat. Lighting Shabbat candles is, if you will, a 'fence' designed to call us back to focusing on Hashem in a devoted way after the demanding schedule of a busy week with its duties, preoccupations and distractions. For the Jewish woman in particular, it is one of the most beautiful of fences.

In Tune with Torah: examining our own hearts this Shabbat to ensure that no trace of 'slavery' to anything still lurks within our souls and to humbly acknowledge that we need reminders, safeguards, protections (fences) for our own good as we seek to follow Hashem with all our heart and soul.

Personal Thoughts

Kedoshim
Vayikra/Leviticus 19:1 – 20:27

Hashem spoke to Moshe, saying, 'Speak to the entire community of Israel and say to them: You must be holy because I, Hashem your L-rd, am holy'. Vayikra/Lev. 19: 1-2

These are the opening words of this parsha and they are followed by numerous instructions outlining how holiness is achieved. Many of the verses in this week's reading have to do with interpersonal relationships for they are in fact the predominant testing ground of our sanctification. We are told, for instance, that we must not lie to one another, nor engage in gossip, nor place a stumbling block in front of the blind. According to verse 18, we must not take our own revenge, neither are we to bear a grudge against another. But the verse doesn't stop there.

For the ending of verse 18 says this: *'You must love your neighbor as yourself. I am Hashem.'* This IS the Torah encapsulated.

Whatever you would not want to happen to you, do not do to others. Whatever is distasteful to you, do not do to someone else. If you do not wish to be robbed, do not steal; if you do not wish to be humiliated, do not embarrass someone else; if you do not want to be slandered, do not slander others and so on. It's really not difficult to understand, is it?

Note that the verse ends with the words, 'I am Hashem' which teaches us something very important. The highest motive for obeying the commandments of Torah is to honor the Holy One of Israel. We choose to love our neighbor as ourself, not based on his or her intrinsic worth -- though every human being is of great value; we choose to love not because the other is lovable necessarily; we choose to love because Hashem is our G-d and He has commanded us to do so.

It is His express will that we should imitate Him and thereby achieve a state of holiness. This means learning that at times we are to speak up and at other times, to be silent; at times we are to give and at other times we are to receive -- humbly and gratefully. Holiness is nothing more and nothing less than growing in our ability to be a mirror image of Hashem's goodness, kindness and love. It is said that anyone who keeps this commandment to love his neighbor as he loves himself is considered to be keeping the entire Torah.

We are also forbidden to seek out mediums or fortunetellers; we are warned against various kinds of mixtures and commanded to avoid sexual sins. In the midst of these prohibitions, there is a positive commandment to show respect to older people -- which includes showing respect towards those 'older' in the ways of Torah, even if they happen to be younger in chronological age. Devout Jews stand when a Torah scholar enters the room because of this specific commandment.

The practice of showing respect to one's elders is not as widespread as it was in times past. Some years ago it was unheard of that a child or a teenager would address an older person by their first name alone. A title of respect always accompanied the person's name, such as Aunt Sarah or Uncle David. If there was no relationship, the terms 'Sir' and 'Ma'am' were often used. Today these practices are considered odd in many places, even archaic.

It used to be that if an older person boarded a public bus, young people would immediately rise to give their seat to the newcomer. This still happens on a fairly regular basis on the buses of Israel but I have traveled extensively in my life and have seen this act of respect largely lacking in other countries, whether on public transportation, in shops and supermarkets, or in airport terminals. Most tragically, the general lack of respect that has invaded society at large has spilled over into the arena of religion and spirituality as well.

To show respect to those older than we are is a commandment of Hashem's Holy Torah. It is not just an 'old-fashioned' practice; it is one of the marks of a person who is serious about honoring Hashem and living according to His Torah. To show respect towards elders is to show respect towards Hashem Himself.

In Tune with Torah: examining ourselves regarding our commitment to specific commandments such as the ones outlined in this week's parsha; to honestly assess our own attitudes and behavior with reference to Hashem's instructions given here and where necessary, to repent and commit to improve.

Personal Thoughts

Emor
Vayikra/Leviticus 21:1 – 24:23

Hashe spoke to Moses telling him to speak to the children of Israel and say to them: There are special times that you must celebrate as sacred holidays to Hashem. The following are My appointed festivals.
Lev. 23:1-2

This week's parsha opens with these words and goes on to describe the biblical festivals which we observe every year; God's festivals, sacred holidays which will exist forever and never be annulled because God has decreed it to be so. The Feasts of Hashem are uniquely special opportunities to connect with Hashem in a dynamic way.

The festivals of God are not just memorials of past events but properly understood, they are profound celebrations for every generation of the very present reality of God's involvement in the life of His people, Israel. For example, sitting at the table for the Pesach Seder just a few days ago, every Jew identified with the dramatic deliverance wrought by the hand of God to free us, not just our forefathers, but us as well from slavery for slavery can take many forms.

The discussion of the festivals begins with the reminder of a previous given instruction: to keep the Shabbat holy. In the Torah, the commandment to observe and safeguard Shabbat is given eight times. The number 8 is significant for it carries a sense of abundance and strength; it reminds us of the covenant for every Jewish male child is circumcised on the 8th day and God spoke with Abraham eight times regarding Covenant.

Shabbat is indeed our weekly celebration of relationship with God, and is marked by cessation from all that occupies us during the week so that we can give our full attention to the awesome God Who has chosen us in His abundant love and made us His own.

Both on Shabbat and on the other festivals - Pesach, Shavuot, Rosh Hashanah, Succot - it is a mitzvah to celebrate - to rejoice together with family and friends and to eat and drink together around the family table in honor of Hashem's goodness. It is also part of the mitzvah to share food with the less fortunate, ensuring that every Jew has what they need to celebrate God's festivals. The Torah tells us that the holidays are to be celebrated as sacred days when no work may be done and that this commandment to celebrate is "an eternal law for all

generations no matter where you live!"
Lev. 23:21

Surely, celebrating the festivals can be considered among the most enjoyable of all the commandments!

But there is also another aspect we must consider. Though we find these holidays most pleasurable for ourselves and thoroughly enjoy time with our family and our friends, let us never forget that these days are meant to bring pleasure to Hashem as well. It's not all about us; it's all about Him.

Each of the appointed festivals are for His pleasure.

What father does not take great delight in seeing His children grateful and joyful? Grateful -- and joyful -- in that order.

Daily living has a way of encroaching on our mental and emotional well being with the unexpected, the frustrating, the annoying, and the exhausting. We too easily lose an abiding sense of thankfulness and succumb all too quickly to complaining and kvetching. We forget that every day is a gift, every breath we take a provision not to be taken for granted. The Festivals of Hashem, rightly observed, bring us back to an attitude of gratitude, one of the healthiest characteristics of the mentally, emotionally, physically and spiritually healthy person. We, of all people, have SO much to be thankful for - every day, in every way.

In Tune with Torah: having a "check up from the neck up". How is our thought life? Does our mind entertain thankful, positive thoughts? Or have we developed a negative, cynical, or depressed outlook? If so, this Shabbat is the time to repent and resolve to nurture within ourselves and our families an ever increasing thankfulness, the key to abiding joy and peace.

Personal Thoughts

Behar
Vayikra/Leviticus 25:1 – 26:2

When your brother becomes impoverished and loses the ability to support himself in the community, you must come to his aid. Help him survive, whether he is a convert or a native Israelite. Lev. 25:35

The Torah is teaching us here that we must be kind to others, in deed and also in thought. We are forbidden to look down on the unfortunate or randomly pass judgment on their difficulties. If a fellow Jew is in dire straits, one should do everything in his power to assist him with money, food, emotional support, whatever is needed.

The comparison is made to seeing a person walking down the street who is swaying from side to side and looks like he is about to fall down. One person may say, "Reach out and hold him up so he doesn't fall in the mud." Another may say, "Why should I do anything now? If he does fall down, I'll help him up." Is it not kinder to keep one from falling, rather than picking him up after he has fallen? For the one who falls is humiliated and perhaps injured and the Torah tells us elsewhere: "Don't embarrass one another" which includes preventing someone from being embarrassed if you have it in your power to do so.

Keeping a brother from falling into abject poverty, or losing his home, his job, etc. is a greater mitzvah than randomly giving charity to the poor for Chazal say that the chronically poor are accustomed to charity and they are no longer ashamed. But a person who has been a family provider, has held a job and paid his bills, who then is 'staggering' is not only suffering the pain of his inability to care for his family but is also deeply troubled and frightened for his wife and children. To help such a one before he hits "rock bottom" is a great mitzvah according to Torah.

The greatest aspect of this mitzvah is helping someone find a job, or giving him a job if one is in the position to do so. Enabling another to work and support himself and his family is the greatest of Jewish mitzvahs for this help is not just for a day or a week but for the future stability of the one presently in need.

God through His Torah wants us to understand that if we have the ability to help someone else and we refuse, we are destroying ourselves with our own hands. For if we show mercy and charity towards others -- and that not just in the matter of money,

but also in our attitude towards those under stress --
God in turn will show mercy and compassion towards
us and will send blessing and success in everything
we do.

Money is one of the most unstable of
commodities. Many who have been very wealthy
have lost everything and found themselves in need
of the help of others. In this world, a man can
never be sure of his wealth. Therefore, the Torah
says, " You shall support him, whether he is a
convert or a native Israelite." The kindness that you
show towards your brother in need is, in reality not a
favor to him; it is a favor to you! For if you act
kindly towards him, God Himself will protect you in
your time of need.

In Tune with Torah: examining our own hearts for
any evidence of stingyness or unwillingness to share
what we have with others. May Hashem help us all
to be of generous spirit, even as He blesses us from
His abundant kindness.

Personal Thoughts

Bechukotai
Vayikra/Leviticus 26:3 – 27:34

Many religions place their basis of faith in far away promises, i.e.. "Have faith in our religion and you will get Heaven."

While Judaism believes in an Afterlife, a World to Come, the Torah makes no promises that are "far away." It makes definitive statements of consequences. This week's portion says, *"If you will follow My decrees and observe My commandments and perform them; then I will provide your rains in their time, and the land will give its produce and the tree of the field will give its fruit. Your threshing will last until the vintage, and the vintage will last until the sowing; you will eat your bread to satiety and you will dwell securely in your land. I will provide peace in the land, and you will lie down with none to frighten you ... I will make you fruitful and increase you..."*

This portion also contains the words of admonition, "If you will not listen to Me and will not perform all of these commandments..." There are seven series of seven punishments each.

Understand that God does not punish for punishment's sake; He wants to get our attention so that we will introspect, recognize our errors and correct our ways. God does not wish to destroy us and will never annul His covenant with us. This is the Almighty's guarantee to the Jewish people: " ... *I will not grow so disgusted with them nor so tired of them that I would destroy them and break My covenant with them, since I am the Lord their God.* (Deut. 26:44-45)

He wants to prevent us from becoming so assimilated that we disappear as a nation. I highly recommend reading Leviticus 26:14 - 45.

Consequences follow every decision we make - both individually and corporately. Nations suffer because of decisions made by their leaders that are contrary to godly principles and values. Children suffer for the improper decisions of their parents, and so on. As adults, we suffer the consequences of decisions that are out of line with Hashem's clear will as stated in His Torah. And tragically, because none of us is an island unto ourselves, our decisions also affect those around us whether we intend that or not.

And when the decisions we have already made, cause dissension or strife between us and others, let the following ten principles guide you in discussion:

Begin with something positive to create a friendly atmosphere.

Appreciate the human being you are talking with. He/she is not the enemy.

Respect your opponent's desire to do the right thing. When possible, give positive feedback.

Earnestly seek peace. If your opponent makes offensive mistakes, don't retaliate, rather help him/her recover.

Be open-minded. If your opponent makes a good objection, admit to it and enjoy your new clarity.

Don't interrupt when others are speaking. Listen respectifully. Treat others as you would like to be treated. In the long term, you will save time.

Don't provoke your opponent by hitting his/her hot buttons.

Stay focused on the point of discussion. Don't destroy the conversation with emotional outbursts.

Lead by example. Don't demand your opponent to keep these rules. You teach them by example.

End by summarizing what you have in common and be willing to compromise where possible for the sake of peace.

In Tune with Torah: As we face day to day decisions, let us be mindful of how each decision will affect those around us and have their best interests at heart, not just our own.

Personal Thoughts

Bamidbar/Numbers

The Fourth Book
Of the Torah

Bamidbar

Bamidbar/Numbers 1:1 - 4:20

We begin now our study of the fourth book of the Torah, Bamidbar (titled in English as Numbers. Bamidbar in Hebrew means 'in the desert'. The English title was apparently taken from the second verse of the book which deals with the numbering of the tribes.

However, the essence of this book is truly captured in this one word, Bamidbar, for the book is about the long sojourn in the desert, and walks us through the winding route taken by the children of Israel on their way to the Promised Land. We remember that this prolonged route was not part of the original plan, but resulted from the sin of the spies. At that point it was decreed that the generation of the spies would wander in the desert, and ultimately perish among the vast dunes of sand.

'And the Lord spoke to Moses and to Aaron, saying, "How long shall I bear this evil congregation, which murmur against me? I have heard the murmurings of the People of Israel, which they murmur against me. Say to them, As truly as I live, said the Lord, as you have spoken in my ears, so will I do to you. Your carcasses shall fall in this

wilderness; and all who were counted of you, according to your whole number, from twenty years old and upward, who have murmured against me, shall by no means come into the land I have sworn to settle you therein, save Caleb the son of Yephunneh, and Joshua the son of Nun.

But your little ones, which you said would be prey, them will I bring in, and they shall know the land which you have despised. But as for you, your carcasses, they shall fall in this wilderness. And your children shall wander in the wilderness forty years, and bear your backslidings, until your carcasses are wasted in the wilderness. According to the number of the days in which you spied the land, forty days, each day for a year, shall you bear your iniquities, forty years, and you shall know my displeasure."
Numbers 14:26-34

Perhaps we would be led to believe that had this defiant sin not taken place, the desert would not be a part of our collective consciousness. However, from the very beginning of the process of the Exodus, Moses is told that the desert, the wilderness, is the destination for the religious experience.

Numerous times in the "negotiations" with Pharaoh the interchange focused on the subject of the desert. When the congregation finally arrives at

Mount Sinai to receive the Torah, again the desert is mentioned: *'In the third month, when the people of Israel were gone forth out of the land of Egypt, the same day came they into the wilderness of Sinai. For they had departed from Rephidim, and had come to the desert of Sinai, and had camped in the wilderness; and there Israel camped before the mount.* (Exodus 19:1-2)

The desert is the scene for the giving of the Torah as it also was a crucial element of the experience of Moses at the Burning Bush. Moses was drawn like a magnet to the place of spiritual revelation, yet we sometimes wonder at the choice of the desert as place of spirituality.

When man was created he was placed in a garden; Eden was a beautiful place, with flowing rivers, lush flora, pleasing to the eye. A more pastoral setting cannot be imagined. And, most importantly, the Spirit of God permeated the entire expanse. Work was unknown, struggle undiscovered. Man and beast lived in unity, idyllic and ideal - paradise.

The desert seems like the very antithesis of Gan Eden: barren and empty, either too warm or too cold, desolate, lifeless. It seems that the only thing in common between the two was the snake for the

Torah describes the desert of the Israelite wanderings as a: *Great and terrible wilderness, where there were venomous serpents, and scorpions, and drought, where there was no water.* (Deut. 8:15)

And this is the epicenter of spirituality?

In the Garden of Eden, when man walked with God, there was no need to work or toil. But man destroyed that world, he hid from his Maker, causing a terrible exile which has lasted through the millennia.

But the desert where supplies are scarce and survival appears doubtful is the perfect place to find God.

Who led you through that great and terrible wilderness, where were venomous serpents, and scorpions, and drought, where there was no water; who brought you water out of the rock of flint. Who fed you in the wilderness with manna, which your fathers knew not, that He might humble you, and that He might test you, to do you good in the end. And you say in your heart, "My power and the might of my hand has gotten me this wealth." And you shall remember the Lord your God; for He is who gives you power to get wealth, that He may establish

His covenant which He swore to your fathers, as it is this day. (Deut. 8:15-18)

The objective of the desert experience was for jaded man to develop more trust in God. The Cloud of Glory, perhaps more than any other symbol, represented their special relationship to God in the desert. Upon the lifting of the cloud they traveled; upon the settling of the cloud they encamped. The cloud was their constant companion, representing Divine faithfulness and care.

And on the day that the Tabernacle was erected the cloud covered the Tabernacle, the Tent of the Testimony; and at the evening there was upon the Tabernacle like the appearance of fire, until the morning. So it was always; the cloud covered it by day, and the appearance of fire by night. And when the cloud was taken up from the tabernacle, then after that the People of Israel journeyed; and in the place where the cloud abode, there the People of Israel pitched their tents. At the commandment of the Lord the People of Israel journeyed, and at the commandment of the Lord they camped; as long as the cloud abode upon the Tabernacle they rested in their tents. And when the cloud remained long upon the Tabernacle many days, then the People of Israel kept the charge of the Lord, and journeyed not. And so it was, when the cloud was a few days upon the

Tabernacle; according to the commandment of the Lord they abode in their tents, and according to the commandment of the Lord they journeyed. ... At the commandment of the Lord they rested in the tents, and at the commandment of the Lord they journeyed; they kept the charge of the Lord, at the commandment of the Lord by the hand of Moses. (Numbers 9:15-23)

And the People of Israel took their journeys out of the wilderness of Sinai; and the cloud rested in the wilderness of Paran. (Numbers 10:12)

Not only did the cloud set the itinerary, but it was intrinsically related to the Tabernacle, always hovering above the structure. For nearly forty years, the cloud and the Tabernacle visibly accompanied the Jews in their travels.

On a contemporary level, we may not literally wander in a physical desert today to achieve an intimacy with Hashem, but certainly everyone who strives for holiness has at one time or another a 'desert' experience which often seems unpleasant and difficult yet is designed to yield the same result in us - a profound trust and closeness to our God.

In Tune with Torah: recognizing our 'desert' times as gifts from on high to spur us on to deeper intimacy with God and greater trust in His all-encompassing faithfulness.

Welcome to the desert!

Personal Thoughts

Naso

Bamibar/Numbers 4:21 – 7:89

This portion is the longest in the Torah and it relates the bringing of offerings by the princes of the tribes of Israel at the dedication of the altar. While the description of each gift fascinates us, for our purposes here, we will look at the last gift brought by the prince of the tribe of Efraim, Elishama ben Amihud. Since the princes began bringing their gifts on the first day of the week, Sunday, we realize that the prince of Efraim brought his gift on Shabbat, as explained in the Midrash.

We remember that when Yaakov blessed his grandsons, Menasheh and Efraim, the sons of Yosef, he gave precedence to the younger, Efraim, over Menasheh, the firstborn. There are many things to learn from this incident, such as the following.

The name of a person reveals much about his essence, and in these two cases, we are given this information explicitly by the Torah: *Yosef named the firstborn Menasheh, "for God has made me forget all of my trouble and all of my father's house."* He named the second Efraim, *"for God has made me fruitful in the land of my oppression."* (Bereishis 41:51-52)

The name, Menasheh, finds its root meaning in forgetting, or distancing oneself from the past. This represents a particular sort of Divine service, in which one divests oneself of all manner of evil deeds and habit patterns from one's youth and radically changes one's lifestyle to pursue righteousness and holiness.

Efraim, on the other hand, finds its root meaning in fruitfulness. This is a different approach toward spiritual goals. While Menasheh's approach is to be consciously repentant of the past and continually seek to rectify it, Efraim's approach is to focus on developing godly character and performing good deeds at every opportunity.

In other words, we could say that Menasheh's approach is somewhat negatively based (maintaining a conscious remembrance of the evils of one's past lifestyle as motivation for doing good) while Efraim's approach is much more positive (seeking good, doing good deeds and though repenting when necessary, not dwelling on the past mistakes.) There is a verse in the psalms which says *"Depart from evil...and do good."* In our context, Menasheh is "depart from evil," whereas Efraim is "do good."

Yaakov's choice to bless Efraim before Menasheh represents choosing a lifestyle in which one first concentrates on performing good deeds. Then, due to the influx of holiness generated by one's new mode of life, any evil traits will automatically dissipate over time. In Yaakov's view, this approach to life was preferable to focusing on overcoming bad behavior before worrying about doing good deeds. And in fact, this is the general rule in Jewish life: we must begin our observance of the Torah by doing and learning, assigning a secondary role to eliminating evil. This will naturally follow later, for the more we acquire a Torah lifestyle, the more rapidly will any negative character traits and/or behavior be replaced by holiness.

In Tune with Torah: renewing our commitment to live the Torah's commandments, choosing to do what is pleasing in Hashem's sight knowing that the end result will be a falling away of negative behaviors.

Personal Thoughts

Be-halot'cha
Bamidbar/Numbers 8:1 – 12:16

Towards the end of this Torah portion God describes Moses as the most humble man upon the face of the earth. According to the Torah's definition of greatness, Moshe represents the ultimate level a person can reach; he attained the greatest closeness to God humanly possible, learned the most Torah and was the teacher of all of the community of Yisrael. It is clear that his outstanding humility is directly connected to his greatness.

We know that there are many desirable character traits such as kindness and honesty. Why is humility the one quality that Hashem highlighted so clearly?

In order to answer this it is instructive to analyze the trait which is the opposite of humility - arrogance. The Talmud describes God's hatred for the arrogant person - God says that there is no room for Himself and the arrogant person to dwell together. Why?

The arrogant person believes that he does not need God to succeed in life. He considers his own talents sufficient and therefore he does not need God's 'help'. Accordingly, God responds measure for measure and complies with this attitude; He withholds from the arrogant person any heavenly help; i.e., God doesn't reside with him. Therefore, sonner or later, the arrogant man/woman is greatly limited in what he/she can achieve on their own. They may be intelligent, but intelligence is only part of the picture - without insight, wisdom and social maturity, the arrogant man eventually fails in one way or another. As written in Mishle (Proverbs), pride goes before a fall.

The humble person has just the opposite attitude. He realizes that his talents are God-given and gives God the appropriate honor for whatever he/she is able to accomplish in life. The person who recognizes that God provides him with whatever ability is necessary, experiences unlimited potential because his source (God) is unlimited. If a person is willing to exert the necessary effort in doing God's will then he can achieve significant success.

This explains why Moses' attribute of humility enabled him to reach such incredible heights. He realized that anything he tried to do was only through the power given to him by God. This recognition removed any limitations on what he could do, and as we see many times in the Torah he attained supernatural achievements.

In Judaism we are taught that everyone is obligated to ask himself when he will reach the level of the Forefathers. "All one's behavior and actions must be directed at reaching the level of the actions of the Holy Forefathers. Even though the distance is extremely far, and according to the normal laws of nature, it is impossible to reach it, nevertheless man is obligated to strive to do whatever he can to attain it." Such ambitious goals for holiness and righteousness can be attained but only through the help of Hashem.

Thus we have seen that humility is the key to greatness. Many years ago I heard a teacher say, "If you truly want to be great in God's eyes, don't wait for opportunities to be thrust upon you to exercise humility. Actively LOOK for opportunities to walk humbly."

In Tune with Torah: this coming week, ask Hashem to help you seize opportunities to voluntarily humble yourself before Him and others.

Personal Thoughts

Shlach
Bamidbar/Numbers 13:1 – 15:41

God speaks to Moses, *"Send forth men to spy out the land of Canaan that I am giving to the Jewish people"* Bamidbar/Numbers 13:2.

We assume that this is the beginning of the story. However, in Parshat Devarim, when Moses reviews the events of the Jewish people's 40 years in the desert, we read: "And you all drew near to me and said, 'Let us send men ahead of us to spy out the land''." Dev./Deut. 1:22. After the people made this request, Moses consulted God to determine what to do, and God allowed the expedition to take place.

As the story progresses, we see that most of the spies return with a negative report about the land. These people subsequently die in a horrific plague. Bamidbar/Numbers 14:37. Obviously, the incident with the spies was considered to be a very serious mistake. How, then, are we to understand this week's Haftorah, in which, 40 years after this incident, Joshua sends spies as well (Joshua 2)?

Aha - notice: the spies in the time of Joshua are not condemned or punished; on the contrary, their behavior is seen as permissible or even commendable. What is the difference between the two situations?

The Slonimer Rebbe, in Netivot Shalom, teaches that Moses and the Jewish people had different reasons for sending spies into the Land.

Moses trusted God completely. He had no doubt that the land was good; he merely wanted to define its energy, to learn how to prepare for it in the best possible way. The Jewish people, on the other hand, had a different motivation. Their faith was weaker than Moses' faith; they were leery of entering unknown territory -- even though it had been Divinely promised to them -- and thus were primarily interested in investigating the physical and material nature of the Land. In other words, they wanted more information before truly committing to doing what Hashem had told them to do. Hmmm - do we ever do that???

Perhaps the real challenge to the spies was whether they should conduct their mission according to Moses' perspective or the people's perspective. Whose agents were they going to be? Would they look at the land through spiritual eyes, like Moses, or would they instead evaluate the Land from the physically oriented perspective of the people?

This whole episode teaches us a valuable lesson. In our own lives, whenever we do a mitzvah, we must ask ourselves WHY we are doing it.

Whose mission are we carrying out? Whose agents do we want to be? Are we doing the mitzvah for ourselves, or for God?

Our focus makes all the difference. If we do a mitzvah for the right reasons, we grow in the right direction. If we do the same mitzvah, but for our own selfish motives (money, power, honor, etc.), we move in the wrong direction.

Now we can understand why Parshat Shlach begins with God's response to the Jewish people, instead of their initial request. Since the people's request is not mentioned, we can learn that the spies were not intended to be guided by the people's motivations. We also catch a hint to this idea in the wording of God's response to Moses,

"Shlach lecha" (literally, "Send for yourself"). The Sages interpret the seemingly superfluous word as meaning "from your [Moses's] perspective."

In other words, God excludes the perspective of the Jewish people from His command, implying that the spies should not go on their mission for the people's "logical" reasons but only as a means of preparing for an act of obedience, which was the motivation of Moses.

This explains why Moses selected spiritual leaders (and not professional spies) for this mission. Moses was not interested in physically spying out the Land; rather, he wanted to investigate the land's spiritual makeup. The best-equipped people for such a task were those steeped in spirituality.

Now we can also understand the difference between the incident with the spies in this week's parsha and the spies who were sent in the time of Joshua. In Parshat Shlach, when the spies return, the Torah tells us, *"The spies came ... to report to the Jewish people"* Bamidbar/Numbers 13:26.

In the time of Joshua, however, the verse tells us that the spies *"came to Joshua and told him all that had happened to them"* (Josh. 2:23). The spies sent by Joshua reported back to him alone. Thus each group by its action upon returning demonstrates to us the overriding motivation of their action.

May we be blessed to go in the ways of the righteous, and follow the ways of God, in order to ensure that all of our actions are done for the right reasons.

In Tune with Torah: examining the motives of our hearts and determining to do all that we do out of love for Hashem - the kind of love that wants to live in obedience to His Torah.

Personal Thoughts

Korach
Bamidbar/Numbers 16:1 – 18:32

Reading the account of Korach's rebellion still astounds me, though I've read it for years now. After all that the children of Israel had experienced to this point, how could anyone question the authority of Moshe? The Sages tend to agree that envy was the motivating factor. Korach wanted position and power and his envy overrode his good sense and understanding, not to mention his spirituality. Envy is indeed a very deadly sin.

When Korach accused Moshe of seizing the leadership, he said, *"Why do you exalt yourself over the congregation of God?"* The Torah continues, *"Moshe heard and fell on his face,"* and afterwards reprimanded Korach. There is a great lesson to be learned here.

Moshe's first reaction at being criticized was to fall on his face, not to lash out at his accuser and mount a defense.

Although Moshe knew that God had appointed him leader over Israel, because of his great humility, his reaction to this accusation was to think that perhaps he had let his position go to his head, perhaps he was in fact guilty of vanity, and even, perhaps, Korach was an agent of God to deliver a well-deserved rebuke. Now that is a humble soul....

Moshe fell on his face to do some serious soul-searching; only after he felt his conscience was clear, did he arise and rebuke Korach.

It's our turn now to do some soul searching. What is our reaction to being criticized - whether it's deserved or not deserved? Is our first impulse to get angry?   To lash out in defense? To justify our ourselves?   To respond with harsh criticism of the other person, reminded them "You're not so perfect yourself, you know."

Constructive criticism should always elicit a positive response from us for it is the only way we can grow and improve ourselves.   Though it's humbling, we must embrace it; in fact, that very feeling of being embarrassed or humbled just proves that our humility is still imperfect.

Where the real virtue shines is when we can be mature enough to respond appropriately to destructive criticism, such as Korach leveled against Moshe. This demonstrates his greatness: he did not reject out of hand the accusation of Korach, but first searched his own soul to see whether there was any validity to it at all.

One cannot live life without experiencing criticism - some justified, some not. The wise person listens even to the unpleasant accusations with a maturity that does as Moshe did -- ponders what was said to see if there is any grain of truth at all contained in the accusation. Though the accuser's intentions may be malicious, what they say could contain an element of truth that we need to hear. Even if 98% of it is incorrect, it is well worth uncovering the 2% for the standard that Hashem has set for us in the Torah is high: *'You shall be holy, as I am holy...'*

The ability to accept criticism graciously, without anger or defensiveness, is the mark of a spiritually mature and truly humble person.

In Tune with Torah: re-examining my reactions to criticism or correction and striving for the kind of humility that will hear truth from even the most unlikely of sources and respond appropriately in order to grow in maturity and wisdom.

Personal Thoughts

Chukat

Bamidbar/Numbers 19:1 – 22:1

"When Og, King of Bashan, went to do battle with Israel, God said to Moshe, 'Do not fear him, for into your hand have I given him'." 21:34

The topic of the merit for good deeds is a fascinating one that has occupied many a study through the ages. We know from the Torah that good deeds bring blessings. Rashi comments on the verse above that Moshe was concerned that Og might be victorious over the Israelites in the merit of his having informed Avraham that his nephew, Lot, had been taken captive. (The "fugitive" in Gen. 14:13 is generally considered to have been this same man, Og)

Rashi also comments, however, that Og's intention may not have been pure. There seems to be some indication that he hoped Avraham might be killed so that he, Og, could marry Sarah. Nevertheless, Avraham wondered if his meritorious deed of enabling Avraham to save his nephew would grant him blessing in battle.

This is one of many examples in Torah of how the patriarchs viewed the merit of doing an act of kindness (chesed). Even if the action is done with ulterior motives, and even if the motive is reprehensible, the very fact that the kindness was shown at all merits at least some reward -- in this case, saving the life of Lot. And you know that in Judaism, saving a life is of the highest priority.

Acts of kindness are inestimably precious in the eyes of God, whose own kindness is boundless and everlasting. Our deeds of kindness give him great pleasure for we are reflecting His nature and emulating Him.

One of the 'temptations', if you will, that comes to all of us is to feel as if "why am I always the one who has to give in?" or "why do I always have to be kind but they're not?" We tend to fall into this trap if we lose perspective on why we do acts of kindness. They are not predicated on the worthiness of the person to whom we show kindness.

We do acts of chesed because we want to be like our Father who is kind to all. We do acts of kindness because it is the RIGHT thing to do. It is not up to us to decide if the person at hand "deserves" our kindness. The truth is that none of us "deserves" the incredible Kindness of our God towards us. We choose kindness because our Father deserves to be honored in this way. That, my friends, is the perspective that will create men and women of holy kindness who will shed light and love wherever they go.

Neither do we decide on acts of kindness depending on what benefit they may bring to us in this life. G-d forbid! That's not kindness but self-serving hypocrisy! May none of us be found there!

In Tune with Torah: examine your kindness quotient. How are you doing? Why are you doing what you do? Can you be kind even to those who are not kind to you? If you can, blessed are you for walking in the ways of the Holy One of Israel!

Personal Thoughts

Balak

Bamidbar/Numbers 22:2 – 25:9

Though named "Balak" after the Moabite king who initiated the dramatic incidents recorded in it, the story itself in this portion really belongs to Bilaam, the prophet Balak hired to curse the Jews and destroy them.

The special weight attached to Bilaam's words can be traced back to Bilaam's exalted status as a prophet; his level of prophecy is considered to be on par with Moses' own in some sense.

Bilaam is compared to Moses because they both managed to connect with God on the highest level but that does not mean they connected in the same fashion. God specifically told Moses to avoid connecting with Him while His anger was on display, while Bilaam was the only person in human history capable of identifying the exact moment of God's anger, and it was this angry aspect of God that he was a specialist in connecting with. Is there any way we can understand the idea of connecting with God's anger a bit more clearly?

The truth is that although we do not realize it, we are all quite familiar with the idea of connecting with God through the power of anger.

Most of us have had the following common spiritual experience. Some traumatic event in our lives causes us to wonder: 'why is this happening to me', and leads us to introspection. Our soul searching leads to the discovery that we are functioning far beneath the level of spirituality that we find acceptable; we suddenly become impatient and angry with ourselves.

Not everyone reacts in the same fashion to such an experience but some people convert the emotional energy of this spiritual impatience and anger into a firm resolution to disassociate from their present social framework and life-style entirely and institute drastic changes in their lives. Bilaam exemplifies the practice of connecting with God more through anger and frustration than any other way. Each time Bilaam searched for contact with the Divine presence, he left Balak and his associates standing over the sacrifice and went off by himself: "stand by your Burnt-offering while I go ... He went alone" (Bamidbar 23:3:); Bilaam's ability to connect with God was only present when he removed himself from others, when his frame of mind was bounded by anger and frustration to a great degree.

A totally different way to connect to God is to reach out through the power of love. The aim of this method is not to escape into a more spiritual realm. The aim is to insert spirituality and closeness to God into every aspect of everyday life. Thus, every activity is dedicated to God with the perception that God is present and watching, even participating by supplying the energy to complete the task at hand.

For the person who follows this path, separation from people is counterproductive to holiness. God created the world for people and gave each person a soul so that he or she can attach him/herself to God. The greater the number of human souls that choose to attach themselves, the more God's presence is manifest in the world and the easier it becomes to attain holiness through the activities of everyday life. Attaching your soul to the soul of others engaged on the same quest enhances your spiritual powers. The highest level of prophetic vision is only available to someone who is a member of a unified loving social group.

Dedicating yourself to this method of connecting to God means dedicating yourself to the elimination of the distance between people to the same degree. The commandment, "Love your fellow as you love yourself," parallels the commandment "Love the Lord your God with all your heart."

In Tune with Torah: to ask "How do I most connect with Hashem? Is it when I'm angry, frustrated, disappointed? Or do I routinely connect with Him from a heart of overflowing love and an attitude of experiencing Him in community with others? The latter is much to be desired and may we all grow in its practice.

Personal Thoughts

Pinchas
Bamidbar/Numbers 25:10 – 30:1

In chapter 27 of this week's portion, Moshe asks Hashem to appoint a successor to him who will go out and come in before the people lest the assembly of Hashem be like sheep who do not have a shepherd to lead them. The primary qualities that Moshe declares for a true leader of Israel are just two: humility and self-sacrifice.

It is written of Yehoshua (Joshua) that he was a man "in whom there was spirit" - how do we understand this as fulfilling the requirements Moshe set forth?

Human beings are created with a body and a spirit. The body produces all of the cravings that stimulate self-gratification, whether in food, physical comfort or other areas of natural pleasure. The spirit is that force that drives us to pursue a higher goal in life. Therefore, these two components of every human being struggle for mastery over the individual. To the degree that the spirit is in control and dominant, to that degree is a person able to sublimate his selfish desires and be dedicated to his purpose, his mission in life.

A self-absorbed person is unable to truly empathize with others. It is written of a very holy Rabbi that at one time in his life, he had to undergo a very painful medical procedure which he endured without uttering one sound. The doctor was astonished and asked the Rabbi how he could keep from crying out. The Rabbi answered, "If I can withstand the pain I feel when someone comes to me for help with a problem and I am unable to help him, surely I can stand this pain for it's far less serious."

The ability to relate to and understand others requires heartfelt empathy. Such empathy is only possible in a person who has learned to rule over his self-serving drives and lives by a his inner person, seeking the higher path of life, the ways of Hashem.

The ability to be a shepherd who cares more for his flock than for himself (whether that "flock" is his immediate family, a congregation, or a group of employees) requires someone who can readily sacrifice his own will, desires and drives in order to care and be fair with everyone in his charge. The first place that this kind of leadership needs to develop is in the home with fathers being exemplary in self-sacrifice and caring for their wives and children for it is a known principle that children learn more by what they experience than by what they're told.

Hashem's response to Moshe is to say, *"Take to yourself Yehoshua, the son of Nun, a man in whom there is spirit."* Over the thirty plus years that Joshua had been the servant of Moshe, he had succeeded in achieving such mastery of his spirit over his physical inclinations that he was a prepared vessel for leadership.

Every person is engaged in the life-long struggle for the spirit to be master over the body, for service to supercede selfishness. Our dignity -- and holiness -- are directly proportional to the degree to which we achieve the dominance of spirit over self-gratification.

In Tune with Torah: sit back for a few moments and think about your general mode of operation with your family and friends. Are you in the habit of acting and reacting for self-gratification or are you improving in putting the needs of others ahead of your own and truly caring about those around you to the point of serving them rather than looking to be served?

Personal Thoughts

Matot

Bamidbar/Numbers 30:2 – 32:42

"The descendants of Reuben and Gad had an extremely large number of animals," the Bible relates in this portion. *"And they saw that the Ya'zer and Gilead areas were good for livestock. The descendants of Gad and Reuben came and presented the following petition to Moses... 'If we have found favor in your eyes, may this land be given to your servants for a possession; do not take us across the Jordan.'"*

Moses becomes extremely upset. He gives them a fiery and dramatic sermon that lasts ten complete verses, a pretty long stretch in biblical narrative. "Shall your brothers go to war while you sit here?" Moses thunders. "Why do you dissuade the heart of the children of Israel from crossing to the land that G-d has given them"?

Forty years earlier, he reminds them, the people of Israel had been poised to enter the land of Canaan. But following a negative report by the spies who were sent to scout the land, the entire nation spurned the land promised to their ancestors as the eternal heritage of Israel. G-d decreed that they remain in the desert for forty years, until that entire generation died out and a new generation prepared to accept the gift and challenge of the Promised Land. And now, said Moses to the Reubenites and the Gadites, you are repeating the sin of the Spies -- a sin which condemned an entire generation and stopped Jewish history in its tracks for forty years. Like your parents before you, you are about to dissuade the heart of your brethren from entering the land. "You will destroy this entire nation," Moses concludes his passionate rebuke.

The Reubenites and Gadites accept Moses' rebuke with grace. In response, they clarify their original position. Far from seeking to free themselves from the impending wars for the Land, they were fully prepared to send their troops into the Land and take a leading role in the battles until they were successfully concluded. Only then would they return to the lands allotted to them in the east. "We will not return to our homes until every Israelite has received his Inheritance," they pledge.

Moses then consents to their plea, changes his tone and grants them the territories they requested.

Several points in this interaction are perplexing.

First, since their intentions it seems, were really pure (they never had in mind to abandon their brethren going to war), how did Moses so totally misread them and become so furious with them?

Why didn't Moses first ask what their intentions were before coming down so hard on them?

Secondly, Moses' accusation focused on the point that it was unacceptable that one segment of Jewry isolate from the rest of the nation, shirking responsibility and escaping the fate of their brethren. But what about the seemingly more important point: G-d wanted the Jews to settle the land at the west of the Jordan! These people decided that they wish to remain on the eastern side. But who gave these two tribes the right to redefine the plan and choose the East instead of the West? Why did Moses in the end consent to their request?

Every serious student of the Hebrew Bible is aware that most biblical plots contain sub-plots (often sub-sub plots), rarely articulated in the narrative explicitly.

This event is no exception: The explicit narrative is about two tribes of Israel concerned with their enormous amount of livestock. Yet the drama in which this episode is captured in the Torah somehow gives one a sense that these tribes were not only concerned about their cattle; something very personal was at stake in their request to remain in Trans-Jordan. What was it?

The Bible gives us no hint. There is no way of knowing. We are left in the dark until Moses is about to leave this world.

In the last section of Deuteronomy, just moments before his passing, Moses speaks to each of the twelve tribes of Israel. His words to the tribe of Gad must be heeded to carefully:

"He [Gad] chose the first portion [of land available], for that is where the lawgiver's plot is hidden."

These brief cryptic words reveal the true reason behind Gad's insistence to settle the territory to the East of the Jordan. Moses, the lawgiver, was destined to die there and never to cross the Jordan. Have you ever considered that Gad wanted to remain with Moses? That Gad could not allow Moses' burial plot to remain isolated [G-d forbid] in the plains of Moab devoid of the presence of even a single Jew? That Gad could not conceive of abandoning, even in death, the one who led them through all those 40 years?

The cry of Gad and Reuben "Do not take us across the Jordan," was a plea not to separate from Moses. If Moses is not destined to cross the river, they too did not wish to cross it. These were no mere farmers worrying about real-estate. These were souls so deeply attached to their leader and teacher that they were determined to spend their lives near the resting place of Moses.

Moses, clearly, did not anticipate such a thing. When Gad and Reuben approached him with their request, they naturally could not communicate the entire truth. They would not talk to Moses about his own death and his gravesite. Instead, they discussed secondary motivations, namely the fate of their abundant cattle.

Moses, in his intuition, felt that what they were expressing to him did not capture the entire story. Moses sensed that their words eclipsed a deeper truth. He thus suspected them in contriving a scheme designed to escape responsibility. Hence, he rebuked them severely.

Yet surprisingly, they accepted Moses' words in grace. The narrative makes it clear that they were not upset by the false accusations Moses thrust upon them. Why not?

Because they knew that they were not being straightforward. Above all, this was not about them and their ego; it was about their selfless love and dedication to Moses. His fury did not alienate them, it merely demonstrated once again the genuine leader Moses was and strengthened their resolve to remain close to him forever.

Moses agreed to fulfill their request. He could not tear himself away from the people he dedicated his life to. If his people reciprocated the love he showered upon them, he would not be the one to expel them from his midst. And at the last moments before his death, he extols Gad for this deeply loving choice.

Nevertheless, their choice is not without criticism from some of the Sages. Notwithstanding the noble and deeply moving intentions of Gad and Reuben, their choice is considered "hasty" and immature. It was emotionally compelling and profoundly moving, but spiritually short sighted for by separating from the rest of the community of Israel and failing to enter into the Land, their own spirituality suffered over time and in fact, they were the first of the tribes to lose their land at the time of the Assyrian conquest.

Yes, Gad and Reuben could not abandon Moses' burial place. They were determined to remain in the proximity of Moses' body. Yet they failed to realize that Moses' true presence would not remain interred in the earth of the plains of Moab. Moses would continue to live on in his vision, in his ideas, in his teachings. And Moses vision was that the Jewish people fulfill their G-d given mandate to enter the Land of Canaan, settle it and transform it into a Holy Land, redefining the physical landscape of the land as an abode for G-dliness.

Moses' life embodied a truth, a vision, a way of looking at the world and understanding the objective of man's journey on this earth. As long as that truth would live in the hearts of people dedicated to Moses' dream of transforming the earthy land of Canaan into a divine landscape, Moses would remain alive.

Certainly to have been in the physical presence of Moses was undoubtedly great. Greater yet, however, is to fulfill his mission to settle the Holy Land.

In Tune with Torah: recognizing the importance of choosing correctly among competing priorities. May Hashem give all of us wisdom to do so in every decision we make.

Personal Thoughts

Masei

Bamidbar/Numbers 33:1 – 36:13

These are the journeys of the Children of Israel...Moshe wrote their goings forth according to their journeys. (33:1-2)

In this parsha, Moshe reviews the routes and encampments of the children of Israel throughout their years in the desert. What is the purpose for this comprehensive review at this point in the Torah?

Each time that Hashem told the Israelites to break camp, the purpose was always to reach a new place that would bring them closer to the ultimate goal: the land of Israel. Sadly, however, we note as we go through the Torah, that while Hashem's intent was progress forward, the people often felt differently. They were frequently dissatisfied with where they were and instead of seeing the next move as forward progress, they simply wanted to wanted to move on out of unhappiness with where they were.

As Moshe begins to recount their travels, he pointedly says that he is reviewing their "goings forth" - their steps toward the goal Hashem gave them -- to reach the Land of Promise. In other words, he is saying, Let me review for you the progress you have made because you haven't truly grasped it. You simply look back and see wanderings from here to there, from one place of restlessness to another. But from Hashem's viewpoint, you need to look back and see each move as progress towards His goal for you.

Now there's a principle for all of us to ponder.

We look back over our own lives and with our limited insight, we sometimes feel that we have 'wasted time' in certain periods or 'made mistakes' in certain decisions. No doubt we have -- BUT -- we need to consider that even in those situations, if our lives are committed to Hashem, He is able to bring us step by step closer to fulfilling the purpose for our lives, even if we cannot see how it all fits together. Even our mistaken judgments or imperfect decisions can be tools in the hands of Hashem to cause our own "goings forth" in life.

Every person who has a goal in life will pause now and then to evaluate what he has accomplished and what yet needs to be done. We are encouraged by the example of many of our Sages who made it a practice each night to review their day before going to bed to assess how they had followed Hashem that day in thought, word and deed.

Before long, we will be entering the Hebrew month of Elul, an annual period of self-examination and repentance during which we prepare our hearts for Rosh Hashana and Yom Kippur. But we do not need to wait for Elul in order to examine our own hearts and behaviors. In fact, we do well to make this a regular practice throughout the year.

So it is in this week's reading with Moshe at the end of the forty years in the desert. The children of Israel are about to enter the Promised Land and he is about to hand over the mantle of leadership to Yehoshua (Joshua). His life mission is about to end and so is the pivotal period in the life of the Israelites known as the time in the desert.

What has been achieved? How are they different now than they were 40, 30, 20, even 10 years earlier? What have they learned? Apparently not enough, for Moshe painstakingly reviews those forty years to insure that the Israelites perceive all that Hashem has done FOR them and IN them to bring them to the goal of possessing the Land He created for them.

If we are serious about achieving a goal in our lives, we must periodically take inventory. In our quest to walk in the ways of Hashem, it is not enough to spiritually 'drift' through life, or simply perform the external obligations. We must go deeper. That is precisely why Moshe reviewed the forty years of experience with the Israelites.

In Tune with Torah: setting aside time for some serious reflection. Have we made progress in righteousness? Can we look back over the past month, the past year and see that we have improved in some area of our attitudes or behaviors? Has our personal relationship with Avinu Malkeinu (our Father, our King) deepened within our soul so that what we do and say flows from our love and passion for Him far more than from simply a routine ritual or tradition? For ritual without relationship is not only hypocrisy, but profoundly displeasing to Hashem, as Isaiah the prophet explained in chapter 58 of his book.

Personal Thoughts

Devarim
Deuteronomy

The Fifth Book
Of the Torah

Devarim

Devarim/Deuteronomy 1:1 – 3:22

The last book of the Torah is Devarim or in English, Deuteronomy.

Seven days before he left this world, Moshe reviewed for the Israelites their forty years in the desert, relating numerous incidents and reminding them of important junctures in their journey -- times and events where the most important lessons were learned.

He spoke these words on the shores of the Jordan which Israel was about to cross to enter the Land of Promise. He would not go with them and knowing well their weaknesses and obstinacy during the time of his leadership, Moshe was very apprehensive that they would stray from the Divine Commandments and lose the Holy Land. In Devarim we find his desperate plea that they not forfeit the magnificent gift Hashem was giving them.

In addition to the warnings, he also gave them his heartfelt blessings for Moshe loved his people intensely. From him we learn the great importance of loving all of Am Yisrael, the people of Israel. Within the community of Israel at large, there are many and varied differences -- differences in traditions between Ashkenazi Jews and Sephardi Jews for instance. There are devout Jews and secular Jews, there are Israeli born Jews and Diaspora Jews (those born and raised outside of Israel). Moshe dealt with all 12 tribes of Israel and each tribe had each unique characteristic and calling within the larger framework of "all" Israel.

It is the same today and from Moshe, and more recently in our history from haRav Kook, we learn that each of us is commanded to love our fellow Jew with all our heart, regardless of any differences between us. Oh that Israel would reach this level of loving one another, even in our day.

In chapter 2, verse 7 we read, *"For G-d, your G-d, was with you; you did not lack a thing."* Despite their wanderings and rebellions, Moshe reminds them that Hashem's kindness was never turned away from them and He provided all that they needed, even when their faith was weak.

Shlomo haMelech (King Solomon) wrote: *"A lover of money will never be satisfied with money."* Eccles. 5:9 This is true not only of money but of all manner of earthly possessions.

We are subject to two major influences: our emotions and our intellect. Our emotions produce infinite appetites, but our intellect teaches us that happiness can never be fully achieved by accumulating "things".

True joy is a quality of heart that arises from a contented spirit. To live a contented life has nothing at all to do with the size of our bank account or the number of our possessions. To live a contented life is to live in the abiding faith that Hashem provides all that we need -- spiritually, physically, emotionally and financially -- and to learn to be supremely thankful for what He has poured into our lives.

In Tune with Torah: renewing our commitment to be a grateful person, thanking Hashem for all of our blessings, taking nothing for granted but recognizing that it all comes from Him -- and making the choice to focus our attention on all that we can be grateful for, and putting aside the mindset of dwelling on what we don't have. May we be a very grateful people as David wrote: "I will bless the L-rd at all times...."

Personal Thoughts

Vaeschanan

Devarim/Deuteronomy 3:23 – 7:11

The tenth and final of the Ten Commandments recorded in this week's portion (Vaeschanan) reads: *"You shall not covet your neighbor's wife; you shall not covet your neighbor's house, nor his field, nor his manservant, nor his maidservant, nor his ox, nor his donkey, and anything that belongs to your neighbor."* (Deuteronomy 5:17; Exodus 20:14).

The structure of the verse seems strange. In the beginning, the Bible specifies seven things we should not covet: "You shall not covet your neighbor's wife; you shall not covet your neighbor's home, nor his field, nor his manservant, nor his maidservant, nor his ox, nor his donkey." But then, at the conclusion of the verse, the Bible states: "And anything that belongs to your neighbor." Why the unnecessary redundancy? Why not just state at the onset "You shall not covet anything that belongs to your neighbor," which would include all of the specifics? And if the Torah does not want to rely on generalizations and wishes to specify details, why does it specify only a few items and then anyhow revert to a generalization, "And anything that belongs to him?

In Hebrew, the word employed for "anything" and "everything" is identical, "Kol." Hence, the above verse can also be translated as, "You shall not covet your neighbor's wife; you shall not covet your neighbor's house, nor his field, nor his manservant, nor his maidservant, nor his ox, nor his donkey, and everything that belongs to your neighbor." By concluding the verse with these words, the Torah is not just instructing us not to covet anything of our neighbor, but also helping us achieve this difficult state of consciousness.

How could you demand from a person not to be jealous? When I walk into your home and observe your living conditions, your cars, your bank accounts, and your general life style, how could I not become envious?

The answer is, "Do not covet everything that belongs to your neighbor." What the Torah is intimating is that it is indeed easy to envy the home and spouse of your neighbor, his servants, his ox and donkey; yet the question you have to ask yourself is, do you covet "everything that belongs to your neighbor?" Are you prepared to assume his or her life completely? To actually become him? Probably not!

You cannot see life as myriads of disjointed events and experiences. You can't pluck out one aspect of somebody's life and state "I wish I could have had his (or her) marriage, his home, his career, his money..." Life is a holistic and integrated experience. Each life, with its blessings and challenges, with its obstacles and opportunities, constitutes a single story, a narrative that begins with birth and ends with death. Every experience in our life represents one chapter of our singular, unique story and we do not have the luxury to pluck out a chapter from someone's story without embracing their entire life-journey.

When you isolate one or a few aspects of someone else's life, it is natural to become envious. But when you become aware of "everything that belongs to your neighbor," your perception is altered. Do you really want to acquire everything that is going on in his or her life?

So the next time you feel yourself coveting the life of the other, ask yourself if you really want to become them.

Ralph Waldo Emerson was correct when he observed that "envy is ignorance."

In Tune with Torah: learning to be thankful on a daily basis for all that Hashem has given us is the greatest protection against jealousy and envy. Being thankful acknowledges that Hashem knows what is best for me and my life and provides accordingly. Do I truly trust Him? That He is doing the best for me? He really is - so let us repent for any jealousy and recognize that though something may "look good" in someone else's life, the truth is that if I had the same thing, it could potentially be the worst thing in my walk with Hashem.

Now *that's* the truth!

Personal Thoughts

Eikev
Devarim/Deuteronomy 7:12 – 11:25

Parshat Eikev begins with a familiar phrasing: *And it will be because you heed these judgments, and safeguard and do them, that the Eternal, your Almighty God shall safeguard and uphold with you the covenant and the mercy which he swore to your fathers.* (Deuteronomy 7:12)

Man is commanded to follow the commandments and to obey the Word of God. This is far from unusual; such statements are to be found many times in the Torah, and in the book of Deuteronomy in particular.

In simple words, could the text just say: When you behave as I have commanded, the desired result will surely follow."

There are different ways to view the observance of mitzvot. Sometimes, certain commandments are neglected because they are perceived as less important.

In the Ethics of the Fathers (Pirkei Avot) however, we are cautioned: ...and be careful with a light precept as with a grave one, for you do not know the (calculation) of reward [for the fulfillment] of the mitzvot. (Mishna Avot 2:1)

A second concern is that mitzvot can be observed out of rote but without proper intention or devotion; these are mitzvot which a person may fulfill out of habit or because 'everybody does it this way' yet have no personal inner commitment to Hashem in the doing of the mitzvot.

A third consideration centers around the intent of the person who fulfills the mitzva: The mitzva is performed, intentionally, but for the wrong reason. Particular deeds can be performed for reasons of altruism, or out of some sort of self-serving motivation but without any inner desire to show one's love for Hashem through obedience. How is such an action to be judged? What is the nature and status of such behavior?

The Sages have written that a mitzva is only a mitzva if the person performing the act believes he was commanded to do so and desires to follow Hashem's command. In the literal sense, the word *mitzva* means "command." It therefore stands to reason that a person who behaves in accordance with a Torah law but does not believe himself to be fulfilling a precise and specific command, is not, in fact, performing a "mitzva."

The question of the intention in fulfilling mitzvot is treated extensively in various Talmudic discussions, but the basic premise is whether or not the person performing the act believes in God and Torah.

We may better understand this in terms of our more familiar relationships: Do behaviors in interpersonal relationships require intentional effort, or is the "bottom line" what is important? If we imagine a husband handing his wife flowers, but telling her at that very moment that he does not, nor has he ever, had any feelings for her, would she still be happy to receive the flowers?

Analogously, the sages of the Talmud debated whether any specific act requires active attention and intention, or if an absent-minded gesture is acceptable. Does the husband buy flowers out of habit? Is that enough of a reason? Or is it truly an act of love and devotion towards his wife?

Rabbi Menachem Twersky, founder of the Chernobyl dynasty (1730-1797) wrote about this in a way that truly resonated with me. He said that the word 'mitzva' connotes more than "command"; he saw within it the word, b'tzavta', which means togetherness and concluded: Every mitzva fulfilled is a point of connection between He who commands and we who are commended and who acquiesce. The result of fulfilling a mitzva is togetherness - what we have referred to elsewhere as 'a rendezvous with God'.

Seen from this perspective, the question is one of closeness, of communication, and there is no communication when the person performing the act does not believe in God, does not believe that God has spoken, does not believe that God takes an interest in human behavior. It is impossible to perform a mitzva if there is no awareness of God's involvement in our lives; as impossible as the sound of one hand clapping, it is just as impossible to have a rendezvous of one.

To embrace Hashem's commandments is a matter of active listening and taking in; not merely passive hearing. We are to forge a powerful, reciprocal, eternal relationship - by accepting God as King and accepting our own role as His servants. The type of listening called for here invites us to be sensitive to even the "minor" commandments, as servants of the King. This type of rapt attention transforms actions that we might well have performed otherwise, or actions that we might otherwise perform without conviction, zeal, or full attention,- into powerful religious experience.

It is this approach to the mitzvot that is our acknowledgement of our relationship with God, and it is this attentiveness that creates the meeting point for our rendezvous with God, Creator and Sustainer of the universe. This attentiveness infuses every act, no matter how small and routine, with supreme significance, for we are in the service of the King.

Every commandment becomes a privilege, a sign of the trust the King has in each of his faithful servants, and an opportunity to repay that trust, deepen that trust, and become worthy of that relationship. That is why we are instructed to hear and listen specifically to the "small," "mundane" mitzvot: When we hear in this way, allowing ourselves to concentrate on the significance of each mitzva with which we have been entrusted and reminding ourselves that these are opportunities to reach out to God who has spoken to us, no commandment will ever seem "small."

In Tune with Torah: adjusting our perspective to recognize that the commandments are not to be 'judged' by our perceptions of their importance or non-importance. It is not WHAT G-d said, but THAT He said it that matters to the one who deeply loves Him.

Personal Thoughts

Re-eh

"See, I present before you today a blessing and a curse..." (Dev. 11:26)

This short sentence has so much to say to us. We are taught that Hashem gives every person the ability to distinguish between right and wrong, between a blessing and a curse. We not only have the intelligence to discern the difference but most importantly, the ability (free will) to make the correct and appropriate choice.

Why, then, do we often make unwise decisions to our own detriment?

Rabbi Twerski says that the reason we do so is because our judgment is distorted by what we would like to believe, not what is actually the reality. This is why, for example, a person will accept the painful process of a surgical procedure to save their lives yet refuse to make the decision to change the behaviors or habits that put their lives in danger - like gluttony, smoking, alcoholism and the like. According to Rabbi Twerski, who is a rabbi and a medical doctor, this is true of every unwise decision. Our thinking is muddled by a distorted perception of reality. Perhaps you've heard someone say, when warned about a danger to their health, "Oh that won't happen to me."

Hashem has set before us a blessing and a curse. There is no middle ground. We need to overcome the blindness of our personal biases, realize our vulnerability to self-deception, and choose His ways at all times.

This principle - that there is no middle ground, only blessing or curse - is taught by our sages. Sforno has written, in fact, "Be cautious that you not be like other peoples who have a middle ground."

How does this play out in our life? Many people tend to think we have mitzvot: things which are obligatory, and sins: things which are forbidden. But in truth, there are many other things we do in life which we might consider 'neutral'.

However, the Torah principle of living is this: *'Know Hashem in all your ways.'* (Mishle 3:6) Having the awareness that we have been put on this earth with a personal mission to accomplish should direct our attention towards fulfillment of our divine purpose - to serve Hashem with all our heart and soul. This requires food and rest in order to have a healthy body with which to serve Hashem. We can enjoy the pleasures of food and sleep as ends in themselves but that would fall short of knowing Hashem in all our ways."

Instead, if we live with the awareness that Hashem has set before us a blessing and a curse, and that He longs for us to choose Life and live, healthy and productive, even our food and our sleep become conscious choices for a higher purpose - to enable us to fulfill our mission in this life.

"See, I have set before you a blessing and a curse..." Which will we choose?

In Tune with Torah: examining our own perspective to see if there be any wilful blindness in our decision making processes and if so, to repent and choose to do all that we do to honor Hashem.

Personal Thoughts

Shoftim
Devarim/Deuteronomy 16:18 – 21:9

This week's portion says that a Jewish king is commanded to write for himself a Torah scroll and to carry it with him at all times. (Deut. 17:18-20).

The idea behind this is that the king needs to maintain perspective. He should remember just where his power comes from, and not make the mistake of thinking that he is in control. In Jewish thinking, arrogance is the worst of all character traits, while humility is the greatest.

The purpose of humility is not so much a hedge against becoming intoxicated with power; rather, the idea is that humility itself is empowering. But how does this work?

Humility does not mean lack of self-esteem nor does it require self-denigration. Judaism's teaching is that humility is a recognition that there are more important things in this world than my own desires and needs. Humility is a matter of perspective. Regardless of one's talents and giftings, humility causes us to realize that the world does not revolve around me. The humble person understands that doing what's right is infinitely more valuable than serving myself.

The more humble, the greater the leader, because a humble person has no interest in his own honor, power and self-aggrandizement. He serves those whom he leads.

In Torah law, the people are not servants of the king; the king is a servant of the people. The first king of Israel, Saul, did not want the job. And because he did not want the job, he was the right man for the job. Here's the bottom line: to the extent that a leader enjoys the trappings of power, to that extent he is no longer focused on serving the people.

The humble person will not only have the confidence of those he leads, he will also be unafraid of those he leads. Doing that which is right for the nation is all that matters to him. Whether or not he is popular is irrelevant.

On a personal level, this applies to us as well. If you have humility, then living with what you believe to be right is more important than what others think of you. A humble person is unaffected by social pressures, unmoved by societal norms. Humility is the foundation of true independence.

Arrogance is a fast track to mediocrity which ultimately leads to failure. Humility, on the other hand, paves the way for greatness. It is no accident that the Torah considers Moses - "the most humble of all" - to be the greatest human being that ever lived.

In Tune with Torah: as we begin the month of Elul, the month of repentance, let us conduct a sincere examination of our own hearts, honestly confronting the reality of how often we do in fact make our own desires and needs more important than serving others.   Let us repent of that selfishness which is an enemy of humility and ask Hashem for His help in mending our ways.

Personal Thoughts

Ki Tetzei

Devarim/Deuteronomy 21:10 – 25:19

You shall observe and carry out what emerges from your lips..." (Deuteronomy 23: 24)

When we think of the commandments of the Torah, this one emerges as a very high priority for in reality, you ARE your word.

It used to be an accepted principle that 'a man's word is his bond' but over time it seems to have become less of a behavioral standard. The word 'promise' has lost the power it once had in the mental attitudes of our society. Promises today are too easily broken. It has become commonplace to make impulsive 'promises'. Sadly, most people today speak with little or no regard for carrying out the words they say to someone else. It's incredible just how often someone will say something with which he has absolutely no intention whatsoever of following through.

Since the Torah is a guidebook for living, how does keeping your word lead to having a happy and fulfilling life? And a life that reflects the goodness of Hashem -- He Who ALWAYS keeps His word!

The answer is that when someone keeps his word, he is emulating His Creator as we are commanded to do in the Torah and that person will actually experience a great amount of pleasure. The reason for this is that a person can only feel good about himself when he makes good choices. Making poor choices inevitably leads to poor self-image, but making positive and healthy choices creates a sense of inner peace and healthy self-esteem, which is what Hashem desires for us.

When you follow through with the most simple of declarations, like "I'll be there at 8:00 PM," it shows that you value your word and what you say is important to you. But here's the thing - the only way you'll care about keeping your word is if you care about living out the truth that you are created in the image and likeness of your Heavenly Father.

When you honor what you say - no matter what it might be - you are actually declaring your faith in the covenant keeping G-d that you love. When you keep your word, you are choosing to make every aspect of your life a reflection of His goodness. When you keep your word, you are demonstrating that you are trustworthy, even as He is trustworthy. The more you do what it is that you say you'll do - even the most simplest of commitments - the more you honor Him and as a result, the better you'll feel about yourself.

In Tune with Torah: renewing our commitment to really pay attention to what we say and resolve to be faithful to every word that comes out of our mouths.

Personal Thoughts

Ki Tavo

Devarim/Deuteronomy 26:1 – 29:8

"It shall be that if you listen to the voice of the Almighty, your God, to observe, to perform all of His commandments that I (Moses) command you this day, then the Almighty, your God, will make you supreme over all nations of the earth. And all of these blessings will come upon you ... if you listen to the voice of the Lord, your God:

"You shall be blessed in the city and in the field. Blessed shall be the fruit of your womb and the fruit of your ground and the fruit of your animals -- the calves of your cattle and the flocks of your sheep and your goats. Blessed shall be your fruit basket and your kneading bowl.

"Blessed shall you be when you come in and blessed shall you be when you go out. The Almighty shall cause your enemies who come to attack you to be struck down before you; on one road they will march towards you and on seven roads they will flee from you.

"The Almighty will command to you this blessing on your storehouses and on all of your actions and you will be blessed in the land that the Lord, your God, gives you. The Almighty will establish you to

Him as a holy people, as He swore to you -- if you will keep the commandments of the Lord, your God, and go in His ways. And then all of the peoples of the earth will see that the name of the Almighty is proclaimed upon you and they will revere you.

"God will give you bountiful goodness, in the fruit of your womb, the fruit of your animals and the fruit of your land -- on the land that the Almighty swore to your forefathers to give to you. God will open for you His good storehouse in heaven to provide proper rain at the right time and to bless everything you do. You will lend to many nations, but you will not borrow.

"And the Almighty will make you a head and not a tail; and you will be only above and not below -- if you will listen to the commandments of the Lord, your God, that I command you this day to guard and to do. And do not stray to the right or to the left from any of the things that I command you this day to go after other gods to worship them." (Deuteronomy 28:1 -14

What amazing promises from G-d to us in this week's Torah portion. We could easily get caught up in the blessings and fail to truly focus on the most important phrase in this entire section: *"If you listen...and perform..."*

Parents rejoice when their children 'listen and perform'. Hashem was delighted when the children of Israel said to Moshe, 'We will do and will will hear.'

The key to enjoying the blessings of Hashem is quite simple: If we listen to Him and do what He asks us to do, His blessings will flow into our lives.

Listening requires focusing our attention on what is being said. A friend of mine was lamenting not long ago about her husband not remembering things she said to him. "Just once," she moaned, "I wish he would stop what he's doing for a minute and really listen to me when I talk to him."

Some years ago there was a song entitled "To Love is to Listen". The depth of our love for Hashem is measured not in feelings but in listening to His Torah and observing it with all our heart -- like a child desirous of pleasing His Father, like a servant desirous of honoring His King, like a spouse who longs to delight the Beloved.

In Tune with Torah: reflecting on our own 'listening' to Hashem this past year, repenting for our inattention and resolving to listen to Him with deepened fervor and commitment.

Personal Thoughts

Nitzavim

Devarim/Deuteronomy 29:9 – 30:20

Jewish tradition teaches us that the judgment on Rosh Hashana concerns the events of this world. As we recite in this majestic prayer:

> On Rosh Hashana will be inscribed and on Yom Kippur will be sealed: how many will pass from the earth and how many will be created; who will live and who will die; who will die at his predestined time and who will die before his time; who by water who by fire; who by sword who by beast; who by famine, who by thirst; ... who will rest and who will wander; who will live in harmony and who will be harassed; who will enjoy tranquility and who will suffer; who will be impoverished and who will be enriched; who will be degraded and who will be exalted.

But although the prayer service informs us about the sorts of matters that are decided on Rosh Hashana, it is less explicit about the considerations that enter the deliberations of the heavenly court. Consequently, it is all too easy to miss the entire point of the day. Not only does such an error result in a missed opportunity, it also opens the door to the possibility of failing to obtain the best possible judgment.

Judgment is a concept related to reward and punishment. Thus, a decree for a trouble-free, healthy life in the coming year represents a reward, while a bad decree that results in poverty and sickness is a punishment.

However, Jewish thinking looks at it differently. Our Sages teach us that it is impossible to receive the full reward for any mitzvah in this world (Talmud, Kidushin, 39b). The reward for any good deed performed by someone with a share in the World to Come (Olam Haba) is received in the future as the payoff in this world is incomparably less. While we do receive blessings from Hashem in this world, as were so eloquently described in last week's portion (Deut. 28), the true reward of the mitzvot we do in this life is reserved for the world to come.

This week's portion includes the following:

Look, I have placed before you today the life and the good, and the death and the evil, that which I command you today, to love the Lord your God, to walk in His ways, to observe His commandments, His decrees, and His ordinances ... But if your heart will stray and you will not listen, and you are led astray, and you prostrate yourselves to strange gods and serve them, I tell you today that you will surely be lost ... I have placed life and death before you, blessing and curse; and you shall choose life so that you will live, you and your offspring... (Deut. 30:15-19)

Hashem gives us the choice between life and good, and death and evil. What we need to understand is that "life and good" ultimately refer to eternal life, a place in the World to Come. In other words, when the Torah tells us, "choose life so that you will live..." it is calling us to make the life choices in our relationship with Hashem, with each other and with this world that reflect our inner conviction about eternal life. Simply stated, Torah is telling us to live our life day to day in the consciousness that this earthly life is temporary and what we do here is preparation for the World to Come.

When we live with this kind of eternal perspective, our day to day life decisions are guided by faith and principle, rather than spur of the moment earthly inclinations. Living conscious of the moment when we will stand before the Almighty One of Israel to give an account of our lives enables us to be much more conscious of even the smallest choice between good and evil, between obedience to Hashem or selfish living.

In Tune with Torah: do my choices reflect an eternal perspective?

Personal Thoughts

Vayeilech

Devarim/Deuteronomy 31:1 – 31:30

Most of the time, Nitzavim and Vayeilech are read together on the same Shabbat and there is an interesting lesson to be learned from that.

Nitzavim means "permanent", "abiding", "enduring", "fixed." Vayeilech, on the other hand, means "movement", "process", "development", "evolution." Some of the sages have suggested that the unity of these two parshiot speaks to us of the Written and Oral Torah.

The Written Torah, recorded in the Chumash, is immutable – or to use the synonyms above – permanent, abiding, enduring and fixed. The Oral Torah is a process, always developing. Since the Written and Oral Torah are inseparable, we are given to understand that even those commandments that seem to be fixed still have a quality of 'evolution' because in every generation new aspects and new insights are revealed during the yearly cycle of Torah study.

In the portion of Vayeilech, the last of the 613 commandments is given: to write the entire Torah. Every king of Israel was required to write his own Torah scroll and even today, it is considered to be one of the greatest mitzvahs to write out the entire Torah. Some Jews make it a year's project from Rosh Hashana to Rosh Hashana or from Shavuot to Shavuot.

We are also taught that those who sing verses of Torah as they learn them will not forget it. Teachers have long used this means in teaching very young children the alphabet for it has been educationally proven that one remembers what one sings, particularly if the song is repeated several times.

Singing the psalms is perhaps more commonplace but let me suggest that we also umdertake the practice of singing verses of Torah. It is a great exercise to do with children and in singing Torah with them, we will also engrave those verses in our own memories.

I have also heard testimonies of people who undertook to memorize large portions of Torah through singing them and discovered that their memories actually improved because of it, a very helpful side benefit!

While it would be most desirable that everyone be able to write their own Torah in perfect Hebrew, in reality that is not possible for everyone who loves Hashem's Torah. Rabbi Nachman of Breslov used to teach his disciples that any of them who were not fluent in Hebrew should pray in their known language so that they could pray with understanding and concentration. I think the same principle holds true here.

If you are not able to write out the Torah in biblical Hebrew, or cannot afford to have a professional scribe (a *sofer)* do it for you, but you have the desire to do this mitzvah for your own personal spiritual growth in the privacy of your home, then by all means, undertake to do so in your known language and as you do, keep your heart open for Hashem to give you fresh insight and illumination with each page that you write. Without a doubt, it is a deeply profitable exercise for our spiritual lives and highly, highly recommended.

In summary, let us use every tool available to us to fill our hearts with Hashem's Torah. Let us sing its verses, let us write its portions, let us discuss it at our Shabbat tables and in our study groups.

In Tune with Torah: let us resolve to employ the various means of internalizing Torah in our hearts that it may produce the fruit of a truly holy life.

Personal Thoughts

Ha'azinu

Devarim/Deuteronomy 32:1 – 32:52

Another Jewish year is coming to an end and with it, the Torah portion cycle with the reading this Shabbat of Ha'azinu. At the end of this week's parsha, Hashem tells Moses to climb the mountain where he will die, "B'etzem Hayom Ha'zeh" — at midday. (Deut. 32:48)

Rashi pointed out in his commentary that this phrase — "B'etzem Hayom Ha'zeh" — appears three times in the Torah:

Noah spent 120 years building his ark. The Midrash says that God wanted Noah to use this time to engage people in discussion about how changing their lifestyle could avoid the coming catastrophe.

Alas, for 120 years, nobody listened, and they ignored Noah's predictions of doom ... until the rain began to fall. They had delayed, procrastinated, and refused to heed the warning signs.

And now with the rain falling, it was too late. That's when people woke up to the reality of what was about to happen. They panicked, and threatened to smash Noah's Ark to prevent him from entering.

At which point, God steps in and says: "I will bring Noah into the ark. Not by sneaking in under the cover of night. But in broad daylight — *B'etzem Hayom Ha'zeh*"(Genesis 7:13).

A similar scene is repeated at the Exodus from Egypt. Despite a year of horrific plagues and endless pleading from Moses, Pharaoh still refuses to let the Jews go ... until the final plague, when a distraught and beaten Pharaoh runs through the streets at midnight, begging the Jews to leave immediately (Exodus 12:31).

God's response? Pharaoh had his chance already. The Jews are instructed to stay indoors all night. They won't sneak away like thieves. Rather they will leave Egypt in broad daylight — *"B'etzem Hayom Ha'zeh"* (Exodus 12:41).

The third instance is in this week's parsha, where Moses is faced with imminent death. "We will not allow Moses to leave us!" the people cried. "We will stop him from ascending the mountain!" Why do the Jews want to stop Moses' death? Because they can not bear to part with their beloved leader, who took them out of Egypt, split the sea, brought water from a rock, and most importantly, taught them Torah.

Imagine that! For 40 years in the desert, the Jews did nothing but complain to Moses. Now all of a sudden everyone changes their mind!

But the die was cast. Says God: "Moses will climb the mountain at midday, in broad daylight — so that all will see there is no stopping God's will."

These three events reflect an unfortunate pattern in human nature. We're reluctant to take action until it's too late. We don't begin diet and exercise until after the heart attack. We don't consider marital counseling until a break-up is imminent. We don't try talking to our children until they've already drifted away and so forth.

We sweep the problem under the rug, hoping it will disappear all by itself. But ignoring it only makes things worse.

So what is the remedy?

Jewish tradition speaks of the need to make a *cheshbon* — a spiritual accounting of profit and loss. Just as a business keeps balance sheets, so too you need a regular system to evaluate your spiritual life. By doing so, we are likely to see potential difficulties brewing, and deal with them now before they become a major problem later.

'Cheshbon' not only safeguards us from mistakes, but also increases our productivity in areas where we already excel.

Here's four simple steps of 'cheshbon':

Ask yourself: "What do I want my life to look like 12 months from now?"
Make a commitment to getting it done this year.
Formulate a plan for how to achieve it.
Ask the Almighty to help you do it.

I know...I know...you're thinking, how many times I've started with good intentions but somehow never quite reached the goal.

A major impediment to growth is the feeling of being overwhelmed by the magnitude of the task. If a goal is too lofty and unattainable, we inevitably fall short and get discouraged.

But the Jewish approach is different. In Jacob's famous dream, God shows him a vision of a ladder reaching toward heaven. Growth, like climbing a ladder, must be one step at a time — in small, incremental goals. The key is to develop a series of realistic, short-term goals, that can be monitored regularly.

To make the plan foolproof, make your initial goal something you know you can reach. Tasting success will bolster your confidence and determination, and you can use this energy to strive for higher goals.

Figure out "step one" toward your long-term goal — and that now becomes your interim short-term goal. After you achieve that, move on to "step two" of the long-term goal — which becomes the new interim short-term goal.

Remember, the longest journey begins with just one step. And since we can't predict the future variables, all we can do is keep moving ahead. One step at a time.

The fact that we may never reach the ultimate long-term goal should not be our primary concern. The long-term goal may seem unattainable, but taking small but consistent steps is all Hashem is asking for. After all, He only gives us one day at a time. If we will take each day as a gift, and make some step each day towards the goal, that pleases Him.

Another key element is to implement a system for monitoring progress.

Every night before going to bed, look back at that day's events, and evaluate your thoughts and behavior. Then make a plan so the next day will be more productive.

Ask yourself:

What have I accomplished today?
Did I accomplish what I intended?
How am I going to improve tomorrow?
What are my strengths and weaknesses?
What's my profit?
What's my loss?
How far have I advanced toward my long-term goal?
What's holding me back from growing more?

It takes discipline to ask these questions, day in and day out. The best method is to set aside 10 minutes of "sacred time" where you will not be disturbed by the telephone, email or pagers. Find a room and lock the door. If necessary, put in some earplugs.

For 10 minutes a day, be alone with yourself, to think, ponder, evaluate and plan.

While Rashi cites three examples of "B'etzem Hayom Ha'zeh," the Torah uses an identical phrase in reference to Yom Kippur (Leviticus 23:29).

What is the connection? On Yom Kippur, the judgment of each Jew is sealed for the coming year. Yet are we prepared, or have we procrastinated? Are we even interested to experience the cleansing power of atonement?

On Yom Kippur, God's will prevails and we are brought to our senses — whether we like it or not. On Yom Kippur, God peels back the mask and we see ourselves in the barest form. No food. No water. No creature comforts. Just a soul and its Creator. The stark reality of our lives... hanging in the balance... in broad daylight... *"B'etzem Hayom Ha'zeh."*

The ten days from Rosh Hashana to Yom Kippur are called the Days of Awe because while we have been focused on repentance for the entire month of Elul, these last ten days leading up to the holiest day of the year, Yom Kippur, commands complete attention, reflection and deep, heart repentance.

In Tune with Torah: Along with family gatherings and celebrations of Rosh Hashana, may each of us also make the time to create our own chesbon and soberly approach Yom Kippur and the new Jewish year with firm resolve to eradicate excuses and procrastination as we dedicate ourselves to truly and profoundly deepen our realtionship with Hashem and pursue holiness with passion in the next 12 months.

Personal Thoughts

Vezot Haberachah
Devarim/Deuteronomy 33:1 – 34:12

In this final portion of the Torah, the death of Moshe is recorded.

And Moshe, servant of God, died there, in the land of Moab, by the word of God. 34:5

The phrase, by the word of God, could also be translated as "by the mouth of God" which is why Rashi comments that Moshe died with a Divine kiss.

Before Moshe's death, Hashem instructed him to ascend to the top of Mount Nebo and from that summit, Hashem showed him all the land of Israel.

Several years ago, I had the opportunity to visit Mount Nebo and stand on the summit in the same general area where Moshe stood. It was an unusually clear day and the panorama before me was breathtaking and overwhelming. I could not help but think of Moshe, seeing the whole land before him and knowing he would not cross over to enter it. He would not have the pleasure of feeling the sacred soil beneath his feet. And why?

Because of disobedience -- a sobering thought.

In the first verse of Devarim 34, it says that Hashem showed Moshe the entire land of Israel "until the yam acharon". The literal meaning is that Hashem enabled Moshe to see the entire country up to and including the Mediterranean Sea.

However, in the Hebrew it is possible to vowelize "yam acharon" (to the last sea) as "yom acharon" which means "to the last day." Therefore, the Sages say that it is equally possible that Hashem showed Moshe the entire history of the Jewish people up until and including "the last day", the coming of the Messiah and the resurrection of the dead. Perhaps this was the compensation to Moshe for not being able to enter the Land at that time. Having seen this, Moshe was re-assured that he would one day enter it, albeit at the end of the age.

It is also very interesting to understand that the name of the mountain on which Moshe died, Nevo, has the numerical value of fifty-eight in Gematria. Another Hebrew word with the same numerical value is "chen" which means "grace".

"Chen" is a very important word in the Torah and is often used with relation to Moshe praying "to find favor" in Hashem's eyes. How precious that at the very end of his life, Hashem chose a mountain whose name is related to "chen", grace and favor. It is a fitting tribute to the entire life of Moshe, the most humble man in all the earth whose life is a marvelous testimony to the reality of grace and our example in every generation.

In Tune with Torah: to draw inspiration and understanding from Moshe's life for our own journey through life. What can we learn from his humility? From his successes and his failures?

Personal Thoughts

About the Author

Sophia Bar Lev has been a teacher of Torah and Tanach for many years and has traveled to more than 30 countries doing so.

She lives in northern Israel and presently teaches a weekly Torah class to English speaking women.

To contact the author, please write to
sophiabarlev@gmail.com

www.ingramcontent.com/pod-product-compliance
Lightning Source LLC
LaVergne TN
LVHW051455080426
835509LV00017B/1764